From the Bestselling Author of **Yes! The Secrets Work!**

Today's

S.O.S.

Secrets of Survival
and Ultimate Victory in Life

Anolia O.

authorHOUSE®

AuthorHouse™
1663 Liberty Drive
Bloomington, IN 47403
www.authorhouse.com
Phone: 1 (800) 839-8640

Although the author and publisher have made every effort to ensure the accuracy and completeness of information contained in this book, we assume no responsibility for errors, inaccuracies, omissions or any inconsistencies herein. Any slights of people or organizations are unintentional. Readers should use their own judgment or consult medical, legal, financial and other experts on the field for specific applications to their individual situations. The author and the publisher specifically disclaim any liability that is incurred from the use or application of the contents of this book.

NKJV
Scripture quotations marked NKJV are taken from the New King James Version. Copyright © 1982 by Thomas Nelson, Inc. Used by permission. All rights reserved.

Published by AuthorHouse 2019

ISBN: 978-1-5246-5453-5 (sc)
ISBN: 978-1-5246-5454-2 (hc)
ISBN: 978-1-5246-5452-8 (e)

Library of Congress Control Number: 2016920634

Print information available on the last page.

Any people depicted in stock imagery provided by Thinkstock are models, and such images are being used for illustrative purposes only. Certain stock imagery © Thinkstock.

This book is printed on acid-free paper.

Because of the dynamic nature of the Internet, any web addresses or links contained in this book may have changed since publication and may no longer be valid. The views expressed in this work are solely those of the author and do not necessarily reflect the views of the publisher, and the publisher hereby disclaims any responsibility for them.

A Gift for You

To: _____

On/For: _____

From: _____

Dedication

This book is dedicated

To all our parents, grandparents, teachers, leaders.
Most especially, it is dedicated to our YOUTH of today
and tomorrow. It is for YOU that this book is written.

Contents

Introduction

Get ready, my Friend! You are about to make your greatest discovery: YOUR LIFE... YOUR SELF! Regardless of the way we feel, life *can* be beautiful, meaningful and fulfilling. Together, we can begin to re-discover what LIFE really is all about and what makes it worth living.

My handy Oxford American dictionary, defines LIFE as *being alive, the ability to function and grow.* Seems like a simple definition, right? But what does "being alive" really mean? Do you ever wonder why there are days when we cannot wait to get up and embrace the world, while at other times we feel empty, like walking zombies going through the motion of life, or feeling like we are merely existing?

There are tremendous efforts being done to better our lives, often at a very high cost. Our *educational system* continues to struggle on what to include in its curriculum. And yet until now, all collective knowledge and technical know-how seems to fall short of meeting the students' needs, especially in preparing them for real life's demands and challenges.

Science continues to amaze us with interesting theories of man's origin and history, along with amazing discoveries and innovations. However, it has remained limited in helping us answer the most vital questions we have about life - what it is and how to live it.

Through analysis, *psychology* has made our lives more complex and interesting, but it has fallen short of solutions to our real problems.

And what about our *political and judicial systems*? There are times when I hear people say, "You don't know who to trust anymore. The real criminals are on the loose, while some innocent people are in jail." Misconduct and corruption are now words we hear to describe our leaders. What has happened to our society?

Hopelessness is prevalent in ongoing news and statistics released by the Department of Health and others. It is astonishing to note that among the top ten leading causes of death in the USA, *suicide ranks above homicide*; meaning, there are more people who resort to killing themselves than people being killed by the others. And this is not only among adults. This dangerous trend is growing among our youth. Despite humankind's efforts toward solutions, the problems remain. Wars, violence and crimes are escalating, many times involving innocent children. Is there really a solution to all this chaos?

Are you ready? This timely and practical book is written to bring LIGHT to life, TRUTH to set us free and HOPE to help us go on. It hopes to bring comfort and encouragement to those who feel depressed, stressed, lonely or empty; courage to those who fear; and strength to those who feel weak, hopeless or that they can't go on. It hopes to bring healing to those who are feeling ill and peace to those longing to forgive or be forgiven.

It hopes to reach those individuals looking for answers: *youth* needing more guidance, *adults* seeking hope in the midst of their broken dreams and *seniors* searching for a reason to keep on living and a way to make their final contributions.

In order to accomplish this, I tell it 'like it is'. No fancy words, but plain, simple, practical and useful words, so you gain insight right away as you read along. For your part, you must keep a total *open mind*, ready to absorb, examine or consider what you are about to discover. A great portion of what you will learn or discover is not commonly taught in our schools. The information is vital but, amazingly, only a very small fraction of the population has access to these valuable secrets. These few individuals either have someone in their circle of family and friends who passed on the valuable information, or like me who had to spend over thirty years and tens of thousands of dollars to gain this treasured knowledge. I feel compelled to share these great secrets which can significantly transform lives, and happy it will now be possible for the mere cost of a book.

My personal search and discovery started when I was in my 20s when I realized that even though I have a professional title, I did not know everything. I still have so much to learn. I must be on the slow side because it took me too long to figure out how to put together all the pieces of puzzle which make up 'LIFE.' For sure, there are still a few pieces left to complete my life's picture, my purpose, but I am now more assured than ever, in spite of all the complexities and challenges that I may still go through, everything is going to be alright.

Now, how about you my friend? How are you doing with your path through life? Remember that each of us is *a story* to be told, a masterpiece-canvass-picture to be shared, which - whether you like it or not - sooner or later could be *a song* to be played or *a movie* to be watched. Isn't that interesting! If you knew this earlier, could you have done a better job? How do you want your life story to be?

Let's begin by asking ourselves this question:

Are you aware of anyone who has not experienced any tough time or challenging situation in his or her life? The answer is clear: No one.

Challenges, obstacles, struggles, tests and trials, whether you like it or not, do come to our lives. These we call "tough times" are natural occurrences in our existence. No one can escape or be exempt from them, not even the most powerful and richest people in the world.

Life in reality is beautiful! In spite of the many challenges we face each day. At the end, life brings powerful lessons to learn from and meaningful memories to treasure.

As we share vital knowledge and relevant stories here, may you find revelations that can help release you from captivities and limitations, help you experience true joy and peace, and finally allow you to live a more productive, meaningful and fulfilling life. To be on your road to true victories.

Today's S.O.S. is dedicated to all parents, educators, our community leaders, state and nation leaders, and everyone else who is concerned with the *quality of life* of individuals, families, communities, and consequently that of our society.

Ultimately, this book is dedicated to OUR YOUTH, our children and grandchildren whom we love so dearly. We need to give our best contribution for their future. After all, they truly are our future.

Yes, life can still be different, exciting and meaningful. It can still be better for each of us, for all of us. Don't let anything or anybody stop you on your road to discovery. Don't let any negative thoughts tell you that you can't, that it is impossible…because YOU CAN!

Find out for yourself how special YOU really are. Discover what life has in store for you by taking the first leap of faith that says, "Yes, I can! I can make it through life!"

Yes, each of us has a chance to have a *happy, healthy and victorious life*, no matter what. Yes, you, too, can survive and live your life to the fullest.

Each of us can make a positive contribution to our society by doing our best for ourselves and being supportive of one another, knowing that in the end, we will all benefit.

Chapter 1

Yes, Let's Celebrate!

When life is going great, CELEBRATE!
When the going gets tough,
the name of the game is SURVIVE!

Yes, You Can!

"*Y*ES!" Just the sound of it is music to our ears. It uplifts our spirits. One simple "Yes!" is enough to assure us, there must be a way. Yes, there is a possible solution! Yes, there is HOPE. Something good is about to happen…

Since childhood, we have been bombarded with the opposing word "No" shaping our negative surroundings. "No, you can't." "No, you can't do that." "No, you can't go… that can't happen." Not that there is anything wrong with the word 'No.' It is a vital word that has to be used when necessary, especially when warning or guiding a child, or imposing a discipline to an adult. Unconsciously, people somehow tend to use it more often than needed. Whether the intention is good, or it was expressed out of habit or reaction, the word 'No' puts a big STOP sign in front of us. And if used carelessly, it can result to a negative effect on us. It is one simple word that when constantly

1

subjected to, and it does not positively challenge us, can slow us down enough to cause us to be less effective and less productive in everything we do.

From here on, we can reject negative thoughts and negative suggestions. We can find means to turn negative news to more positive, productive, meaningful news. We can turn our lives around by consciously making a decision and determination to create a healthier, more beautiful and purposeful environment.

Yes, let's celebrate the GOOD NEWS! Begin right now. Feel the sensation of a new beginning with the word "YES!" vibrating in every fiber of your body. Say it repeatedly. Can you feel it? Breathe with the word, filling your lungs, and allow the sensation to move you to get up from wherever you are. And as you stand, or make a motion as you please, treat yourself with the best "YES!" shout you have ever had. Celebrate because you are ready to face this world. You are ready to face whatever situation or circumstance you have in front of you. You are ready to say "YES to LIFE!" And YES, YOU are here to be VICTORIOUS!

Born to WIN! I first heard of such powerful phrase from beloved Zig Ziglar, one of my favorite life mentors or coaches. This inspired me more as I've somehow felt that way. It's a great confirmation. Let me share with you here that it is true.

Sure, life is full of risks. To be completely shielded from hurt, harm, or loss is close to impossible. However, you can prevent a lot of it by taking proper and healthy precautions. After all, *preventive* is far better and less costly than curative. However, being overcautious is not healthy either. It can paralyze us to the point of inaction. We all know that through personal experience, we do something and later say something like, "I could have..." "If only..." "How I wish I did." Well, from now on, let's not wish our life away anymore.

Now, are you still saying to yourself you cannot, or are you ready to TAKE A STAND and say, "Yes, I will. I know I can!" I assure you that when you are ready, you surely CAN. Practice your "Yes!" celebration each day and feel your enthusiasm and energy spring you to do things more effectively and constructively. Imagine how this simple practice can positively affect your life, your relationship with others, your career or work, and your future. Think of the possibilities. Think of how this kind of attitude can enhance your ability to survive life's challenges.

If you say that your situation is *different, more complicated* or *more difficult,* then let me share with you a conversation I had with my three precious children.

Cristern was seven, Grace Ann was six, and Genesa was five when they gathered around me on our bed one evening. They asked that I tell them some stories. Not knowing too many stories, I couldn't instantly give them one. Then I thought of something that they may be interested in, and I could easily relate since it was a true experience. So I asked, "Would you like to hear how you were born?" I got an instant enthusiastic response, "Yeah!"

The birth of my children was among the most wonderful events in my life. Telling them the story was a true delight. I started with my eldest son. I told them how I carried this beautiful child in my tummy for nine months, while giving him a lot of love and healthy food as he grew inside. I prayed that the baby would be healthy and normal. I shared the rush to the hospital, the twelve hours of labor (I was told), and that Daddy was there, too, holding Mommy's hands while Mommy was having contraction pains. They asked if it hurt and I said "Yes," but assured them that it was immediately relieved and forgotten as soon as that beautiful baby came out and I heard the loud cry. I even tried to demonstrate the big, loud cry of Cristern. They were all laughing. One of the girls asked my boy, "Why were you crying so loud?"

The story I am sharing with you is ordinary, but my son's response to his sister's question was not. His answer was, "Oh, it hurt! I was so squashed," as he made all the facial expressions. I was stunned... did he actually remember? I couldn't help but ask him. He simply said, "It just came to me," and repeated, "Oh, it hurt!" Concerned, I asked him, "But are you all right now?" He replied, "Oh, yeah!" Then in unison, the three said, "Tell us more!" And to their delight, up until bedtime, I went on with the rest of the stories about each of them.

My son's response struck me the most, because it brought new light to a lot of things about our life. When I was still a nursing student, we often discussed labor and delivery. Our talks mostly focused on the mother's experiences while carrying and delivering the baby. I heard several times, from different people, that labor pain is the worst pain that can ever be experienced. And we often wondered why scared young girls ended up getting married and continued to have babies anyway.

When I was in labor with Cristern, it was so painful that my husband told me I kept saying, "No more, no more." Yet, I was in the same labor room the next year with the same doctor, and I said the same thing again. The following year, the same room, the same doctor... but this time I shut up. My thoughts were centered on the beauty of babies, the fact that they are WORTH all the trouble of pregnancy and the pains of labor and delivery.

But what about the baby? As students, we mainly learned about the fetus development in the mother's womb and the infant's growth after delivery. Why was the baby crying? I never really gave it much thought, because based on our textbooks and lectures, the explanation was that it is the baby's first gasp of air. When the baby cries immediately, the health team usually cheers as it indicates that the baby is likely to be healthy and able to breathe on his/her own. If the infant fails to cry and turns blue, it is indicative of a problem. It could be a minor one that can easily be corrected by simple suctioning, oxygen, or further stimulation; or it may mean a much more complicated problem or condition.

After my child's simple comment from a child's point of view, it just seemed to make sense. Knowing how tender and delicate an infant's head is, and being pushed and squeezed at every contraction, for many minutes to get out of such a small opening, gosh, you have to understand what these babies have to go through. In fact, what each of us had to go through! If it was me, I could just imagine being so blue, shocked and distressed that I would not be able to cry right away. I would then be stirred by a gentle slap on my bottom by a caring doctor (my very first spanking, mind you), and cry my loudest cry. What a way to be welcomed into this world! This whole picture, sparked from the words of my son, taught me a lot and has become symbolic of so many things in our life.

When a baby is born, it is always a very special occasion. So far, I have not heard anybody say to the mother or the baby, "Oh, I am sorry that you had to go through such a horrible situation." Never. On the contrary, it is usually a big celebration. Parents are congratulated and the baby is showered with gifts. That's always been our practice. Now that we have a better understanding of what both the mother and infant have to go through, they definitely deserve those congratulations - for a job well done! The gifts that accompany everyone's best wishes are rewards for their efforts and willingness to accept the struggles and challenges of a new beginning. It is a very meaningful victory, well deserving of recognition and celebration.

It is so evident from this that pain and struggle, as much as joy and tranquility, have always been a natural part of us from birth. If you and I, as very fragile, defenseless, helpless infants who have no understanding of anything yet, were *able to survive,* does this not say we are naturally EQUIPPED for survival? And as we mature, shouldn't we be much more capable of survival and have better control over our lives?

Finally, the crying baby (and we now know why) who has just been through the worst pressure and most stressful situation imaginable, will almost immediately quiet down as soon as placed on the mother's arms, as she whispers, "My baby, my beautiful baby. It is okay!" "It is all right!" And after several days of much needed rest, sleep, and cuddling to heal and recover, this precious child is now ready to entertain the world with innocent winks, smiles and motions. And the more the baby smiles, the more rewards he or she gets.

Isn't that just how our life is? Think about that for a few moments. Then ask yourself these questions: What does this important event symbolize to me? What teaching in life can I learn from it? Is there anything more difficult than what I've already been through in childbirth that I cannot tackle now?

If you survived once, you can survive again. If others can, so can you. Just begin by saying again, "YES! YES, I CAN!" "After surviving the ordeal of childbirth, we can declare, "THE BEST OF LIFE IS YET TO COME!"

Discover the Real YOU!

Do you know who you really are? The real YOU? I want you to go to the mirror right now and look at yourself. Now, can you tell who you are by what you see in that mirror? Do you like what you see? Do you like the person facing you? Who is that anyway? Is that really YOU? No, I am not just talking about the face or body that you can see. Now, look again. Closer or farther, have a real good view of yourself. (If you have not done it yet, you will really appreciate this important exercise more if you get up and actually go stand in front of a mirror).

Let's do this again. Ready? Now, come closer to the mirror. It's like being 'face-to-face' with someone. What do you see? You are now face to face with the hidden YOU. What am I talking about? Look at your *eyes* for a moment. Are you beginning to have an interaction with somebody there? (Go ahead.) Next, SMILE! Yes, please, just follow along, because this will be a an interesting exercise. Remember, you are trying to make a discovery here, maybe one of the greatest discoveries you will ever make, if not the most important, long overdue discovery. Again, SMILE, the best, most beautiful smile you have. Do you like what you see in the mirror?

For a moment, focus on looking at your eyes, continue looking if there's a conversation happening. Eventually, you will notice that the way you perceive or see yourself seems to be changing somehow. Now, make faces, all kinds of faces; have fun with yourself or the inner you, laugh if you want. It is OK. As you get more acquainted and comfortable with the INNER YOU, the stronger and better the person you will become. Why? Because you will not be like people who merely exist, like walking zombies, those who look like lifeless physical bodies, looking or feeling EMPTY inside. It is because you will begin to have a more in-depth understanding of your WHOLE BEING. You will begin to discover the Total YOU. The Real YOU with not only be a physical body but also a spirit, a mind, and a full-range of emotion as well. You will be a person who continuously relates with others and the universe. YOU is not just about muscles and bones, face and color, cells and DNA and all these physical things that can be looked at, tested and examined - YOU are a lot more than that.

Now, as we go along, you will discover unseen, undiscovered and difficult to explain phenomena. We do appreciate our scientist who dedicated time and effort to finding answers and explanations, and have satisfied or stirred our curious minds.

Let's pause and ponder for a moment. Did you make a discovery? Did you discover the inner YOU, the one that is beyond the physical body and face that you and the others can see? If you did, that is great! If you don't know what I am talking about at this point, just read on and try to do the exercise again later - this simple formula may help...

What You **THINK** → You **FEEL** → You **MANIFEST** or **REALIZE**

Let's do the exercise one more time. If you really want to learn and master THE SECRETS about you, and you really want to get good result out of this, then first follow these simple instructions:

First, THINK that you are sad, or think of something that makes you sad. Look at the mirror. Do you FEEL sadness? What do you see? Do you LOOK sad? What happens when you are sad? Just because you THOUGHT of sadness, almost instantly you FEEL it, and suddenly sadness is MANIFESTING itself in your face and slumped body.

Now, THINK that you are HAPPY! Think of something that makes you happy. Look at the mirror. Do you FEEL and LOOK happy? Did you notice that you have a smile on your face, your body is straighter, and you look much better? See, Peter Pan has to think of happy thoughts to be able to FLY. In the same way that actors simply have to THINK and FEEL their role, FEEL and presto, they can switch from crying to laughing any time. Boxers, sports players, performers have to CONDITION their MIND before going into the arena. If not, they will get knocked down right away. You set your mind on what you want to accomplish, and the feeling that follows will spring you into action, to manifesting or realizing your desires. It's that simple. So, keep thinking GOOD THOUGHTS.

The real YOU is more beautiful and capable, is bigger and stronger than what you physically see in that mirror. What is inside you need to be discovered, recognized, acknowledged and nurtured in order for you to become the best that you can be, in order for you to reach your fullest potential. YOUR LIFE, once again, can be even more meaningful and exciting when you recognize that you are not limited by what you can see in the mirror but, rather by what you can see in your mind and feel in your heart. You will only look like a WINNER when you have the mind and the heart of A CHAMPION. You will discover that you, your universe, and your potential truly are UNLIMITED! All you need now is to BELIEVE, to ACT on what you believe and to LIVE your life to your fullest potential. Then, you will see your goals accomplished, your dreams realized. You will be at PEACE with yourself and with others. You will experience true JOY. These two main ingredients will keep you in the best HEALTH... which already makes you not just rich, but wealthy in every way! Having all that is LIVING, ABUNDANT LIVING!

Hold on, you are not done yet, in fact, this is just the beginning of your greatest discovery of the REAL YOU! It will get more exciting, like a great adventure, as we go along. Make sure you eat good food, and get good rest and good exercise as we continue because you will need plenty of energy and stamina for this great life journey. Now, let me share some insights through...

My Personal SELF Discovery

Although I have read countless books in my life, what helped me most in my self-discovery is what I call "The Book of Life," It is referred to as the Bible, but I see too many books using that title on "everything you need to know" or "how-to" type of books, so for my own differentiation I prefer to call it The Book of Life or "The Living Words." And that is well-fitting name because, of the many books that I have read, this one has such distinction in providing answers to the questions I have about LIFE, such as better understanding of my life and the lives of others, and how to best live life in this very complex and challenging world of ours. I found this book to be like a complete library, with all the answers to every question I have - everything is in this amazing book. How could one modestly sized book cover everything from the beginning to the end of this world, from the time I was conceived to my final destiny? How could it cover everything from the way I should live my life to how to build relationships, to how to be healthy, happy and successful in life? It also helped me understand that I, like everyone else who will pass this earth, will go through life's many tests, trials and tribulations. Yet it has also given me great comfort and insights not only on how to deal with these challenges as they come up, but also on how to come out victorious.

I have to give The Book of Life the full credit because I once came to a realization that, as human, I have my weaknesses and limits. I have to admit that life is sometimes too tough, more than I can bear, but the knowledge that I am not just an insignificant human being, and the comfort that I get from God's promises to His people, His children, and to me have helped me press on in those times when I most needed help. I could have given up long time ago, numerous times, but this book kept me going. It taught me and helped me to never give up. I am truly grateful for this. Can you imagine if I had missed out on all the wonderful things I have experienced later after the deadly hurricanes of my life were over? I would have missed out on the beautiful endings ahead of me, living my life's purpose according to God's master plan.

Nowadays, more and more people are finding LIFE to be too tough or too stressful to live, and at times it could be too lonely out there. After my long journey through life, having my own fair share of life's ups and downs and witnessing many people from all walks of life out there, I now concluded: More than ever, *"People need to connect with God."* GOD, also referred to as "The Higher Power" or "The Most High," is the ultimate answer, The One WHO CAN provide the ways and means, to everything we need in this life. The Book of Life is the main connection we have to get to know God better, His ways, and His marvelous love for each of us, for all of us.

Next, I have to give credit to so many people and groups: true friends, churches who cared, and those special people, groups and companies that I acknowledged at the beginning and the ending portion of this book, who all gave me and my family the support we needed, and allowed me to witness, verify and experience the truth and reality of The Book of Life. I have also found it amazing that the nuggets of wisdom, the quotes, the stories and sayings that I heard from the elders of my youth, are all based on this book. If you already have this book, then you know what I am talking about. If you have one and have not opened it yet, or if you have no copy of this book, then get a hold of one and start making your amazing discoveries as you are riding on, surviving or enjoying your journey through life.

You are Wonderfully Created, Marvelously Unique

Yes! You are not just 'anybody.' You are not just 'any average and ordinary Jane or Joe.' You are not even just 'special'. You are a way more than that! Do you know that:

- Mankind, including you and I, was created in God's image, in His likeness. He even gave man His own 'breath' of life.
- God knew you while you were still 'being formed'.
- God knows you 'by name', and everything else about you.
- God knows the 'very number of your hair'.
- No two individuals are exactly alike. Proof: No two individuals have the same fingerprints.

"Specially made,'" yes, that's what YOU, I and each of US are. It became very clear that God has planned for each of us to be part of Him from the very beginning. Of all His creations, we are the only one He created in His own image and gave His own breath of life. When you were being formed in your mother's womb, before you were even born, God already knew you and had plan for you. As I write this portion, I have just made a startling discovery: Although some people are fixated or absorbed with the thought that "I am just an accident," when it comes to God, no one is an accident. Anyone of you who think your parents had impulsive, sudden, unplanned sex, or spontaneously made love, actually thinking of you, or for the purpose of making you? What do you think? This is amazing! Our parents don't think about us or know about us until we are already formed, a few weeks or months later, when they get a positive result on the pregnancy test. I am grateful to that first reference we get, POSITIVE! God, who knows about us, from the time we are being conceived or formed, is our true Creator. Our beloved parents are the blessed vessels provided to bring us into this world and nurture us, until we ALL go back home to our true Father and Creator. When it is your turn to experience what it is like to bring a child into this world, then you will have a better appreciation and love for your given parents. The sooner you can love and care for your parents, the more blessings will flow to you.

The last point, about the unique fingerprint each of us has, is to prove to you that each and every one of us is totally unique. There is nobody else exactly like any one of us. Of the billions of people in this world, whose fingerprints have been taken, no two individuals have the same exact fingerprints - not even identical twins are exactly alike or share same fingerprints. Isn't that interesting? Another point, actually, is the use of DNA to uniquely identify each of us, which is, of course, more complicated to explain, so we will not even make an attempt to discuss it here. These facts simply prove that it is TRUE how special we are to God, that GOD CAN SINGLE US OUT from the rest of the population. Isn't that amazing?!

For me personally, what's even greater is my faith and knowledge that the owner of this entire universe who loves us so much is MY FATHER and I am HIS CHILD. The GOOD NEWS is: you and anyone else can believe and claim that, too, if you want to. Can you imagine what that makes US? YOU? I have faith, but I used to get bogged down feeling like nobody at times. But after confirming all these things, I feel more like a CONQUEROR. The universe is for us to conquer, according to His will and purpose for us. Are you ready for more?

Chapter 2

Yes, You Can Be Happy and Healthy

*"Most people are about as happy as they
make up their minds to be."*
– Abraham Lincoln, President of the United States of America

𝒴es! You can be HAPPY! Yes! You can be HEALTHY... in all areas
of your life!

Really? Who would not want that? But with the way things are today,
most people feel that, being happy and healthy is getting farther to

14

reach. Nowadays, more and more people feel defeated, victimized, cheated, or taken advantage of. They lack hope and vision of the future.

Although desirable, the thought of *being healthy, happy, successful and victorious* becomes unreal. It seems more of *impossible than possible.*

I remember during previous periods of tough times, I had some of those same feelings. I was the first to say, "Don't talk to me about such nonsense!"

Is it really nonsense? Is it really impossible?

I would probably still feel that way had I not had the opportunity to personally meet some people that are actually living that kind of life – both healthy and happy. These people have taught me that it is not nonsense, and that it is not impossible. Those special people, for me, have been a great discovery - like finding a gold mine. For me, it has been like discovering the key to LIFE itself, its secrets and answers.

Yes, it really is possible. And as I share with you some of life's treasures, I hope that you, too, will discover your own treasures. I hope that you, too, can experience such a marvelous life for yourself. The true treasures in life are just waiting to be discovered by you and be shared with others.

By the end of this chapter, you will discover that life is more than just getting up each day, going to work, making money, coming home tired, eating and sleeping... just to get up the next morning and do it all over again. You will learn that survival is not the only game to be played. As in sports, in life we are part of a playing team – The Winning Team, actively participating to have a chance to score a big one. This chapter aims to provide you with the knowledge and insights needed to be better prepared to face life and tackle your problems or difficult situations. It hopes to better equip you by teaching how to become more PHYSICALLY fit, MENTALLY equipped, EMOTIONALLY stable, SPIRITUALLY filled, SOCIALLY adaptable, and FINANCIALLY secure as a "healthy WHOLE-BEING."

15

The Secrets to Total Health and Well-being

You may have all the money in the world, but what is it for if you are not healthy and happy?

But what is "happiness" anyway? Is it being in this age of ultra-modern technology which aims to gain us access to all comfort and conveniences; where everything we need and want are supposedly available? Ironically, *happiness* is a word still highly sought after, remaining on many peoples' list as still *undiscovered* and *unrealized*.

People naturally have various definitions of what happiness is. To some, it is "having everything they have ever *wanted*." To others, it is simply "having everything they have ever *needed*." And still, others it is "everything they ever *wished* for." We all, of course, have different ideas as to what we want, need, or wish.

Since I have found that most people believe that *being* HEALTHY *brings* HAPPINESS, we will start there. If health brings happiness, and being happy is definitely healthy, then this cycle puts us on the right track. By the way, do you know that experts on success have found that a healthy, happy person has a better chance to succeed? That should not be surprising.

So, just what does "healthy" really mean? Some people think that if they just stick to their ideal weight, that's healthy. In America, people spend billions of dollars yearly in search of the perfect, healthy, beautiful body. People buy expensive machines and gadgets to exercise and stay fit or attend spas and clinics to stay young and beautiful. But why is it then, that there are countless numbers of successful businessmen, movie stars, athletes, wealthy men and gorgeous women, who have everything that money can buy, but are still lonely, empty, and miserable? I do not need to name them. We read about them in newspapers and see them on TV everyday. Some become involved in drugs, some go through painful divorces, and others commit suicide. It is sad. What has happened to them?

Over the years, I have come to this conclusion: When people are healthy, they are happy. People who are experiencing some sort of health problems are unhappy. If the health problem is not resolved, it makes the person more susceptible to more problems or unhappy situations. So...

How do we know when someone is NOT TOTALLY WELL?

Let's take this simple test again and gauge for a moment your knowledge of *health* and *total well-being*. Check the items you believe are signs and symptoms of health problems.

_____elevated or abnormal temperature
_____difficulty of breathing
_____persistent chest discomfort/pain
_____not eating or overeating
_____smoking
_____drunkenness
_____exhibiting obscene or violent behaviors
_____compulsive gambling
_____drug use
_____can't seem to think straight, very distracted or disturbed
_____worrying too much or always afraid
_____feeling so stressed out or burned out
_____depressed for a long period of time

This should be an easy test, right? How many people actually realize that each and every one of these are actual signs or symptoms of health problems? In fact, these are but a few of a very long list of signs and symptoms indicative of an *unhealthy state* of a person. The overall number and severity of symptoms in turn, become a reflection of the health status of *a society.*

Symptoms like fever, breathing difficulties or severe pain can easily tell us that *something is wrong* and can alarm us enough to seek a doctor or go to a hospital. On the other hand, there are some people who do not even realize their own symptoms, and who are likely to deny that they have any health problems at all. When I see someone smoking, I do not just see a person who is a candidate for lung cancer. The main thing that comes to my mind is, "There must be a reason why this person has to smoke."

If you, or someone you know who comes to mind right now, happen to exhibit any of the symptoms on the list (regardless of number), it is time for some *self-evaluation*. As you progress in this book, you'll be better able to identify specific problems and needs, possible sources or factors affecting them and what can be done about them. Depending on the mildness or severity of the problem, coping ability, and available resources of help, one may be able to resolve them on his/her own, or need to seek professional help, or a combination of the two. Still the *decision* and determination to recover from any health problem rests mainly on the individual.

Let me share with you some basic information I have incorporated into my individual and group health teachings. You may find it helpful for yourself personally or someone else. It is nothing new; it is just not well known or applied.

A Simple Exercise. It's the end of the year and you are getting ready to face the new year. How do you celebrate and prepare for the New Year? Do you make the typical New Year's resolutions, writing down some goals or wishes to accomplish, or do you do nothing, as if it is just another day, just another year? Today is a new year, a new beginning, and you have chosen this time to write down your goals and wishes for the coming year. For the exercise, get yourself a pen or pencil.

Below are seven choices. Number them from 1 to 7, according to their *priority* or *importance* to you (Feel free to add some of your own):

___ Lose weight	___ Better pay/more money
___ New car	___ Better relationship with family
___ New/own house	___ Better relationship with God
___ Be happier	___ Better relationship with others
___ Be healthy	Others:_____
___ Another job/new career	

Do you realize that your answers to this exercise actually determine your present state of health, state of happiness, priorities in life, and how your new year (or future) is going to be? In fact, you have just identified your specific weaknesses and needs as well. This is the first step to achieving your goals and wishes. It is a good start. Now you know what you need to improve, and want you want to achieve. If you write nothing, you have nothing to work for or look forward to. Life will just be "Que sera, sera, Whatever will be, will be."

After reading this book, go back to this page and double check your answers. Will your goals be the same or will they need some modification? What's important, is that you took the first step towards your goal.

How do we attain health to be happy?

Being a nurse has been a great advantage for me. I learned early on what "health" really meant and how to attain it. It means *being well* or *a state of well-being*, simple words with very broad, complex meaning. As I share with you the true nature of health and well-being, you will find that it is not just about ideal body weight, or a good diet, or even a terrific fitness program. It is a lot more than just that.

As a nurse, I learned that when I take care of a patient, I was not only to care for the broken leg or burned arm, fever or pain. I had to care for an individual's PHYSICAL, MENTAL, EMOTIONAL, SPIRITUAL and SOCIAL WELL-BEING as well.

19

For example: A football player comes to a hospital for a serious spinal injury. While the medical staff's initial priority is to stabilize his physical condition, their next immediate consideration is the mental and emotional impact of his condition. Furthermore, there are the social considerations and spiritual counseling if so desired. For someone who is not that strong and who is left alone, the situation can be devastating. At this time, family and friends are usually the best sources of support for him. They are the major factors influencing his speedy recovery.

Let it be known that *an individual* is made up of integrated parts that cannot be separated from each other, nor ignored or disregarded. **Each of these parts is uniquely important and has to be considered as an inseparable part of one's WHOLE-BEING.** That is why when we focus on just one or two of those parts, we usually end up feeling that we are missing something, or our life is not complete. We can always tell when we are not completely well, or not all-together.

As I became aware of just how much our economic or financial situation affect us, I added another very important aspect to my view of life and well-being. I modified my definition of HEALTH as "to care for and to meet an individual's PHYSICAL, MENTAL, EMOTIONAL, SPIRITUAL, SOCIAL and FINANCIAL needs, for his/her TOTAL WELL-BEING." Does one really have to wait until he becomes a patient for his whole being to be considered? Why was I not aware of this concept until I was midway through college? Realizing that not many people understand this concept of *whole being*, it is too important to disregard. So I will pass it on to you.

It is quite unfortunate that we are living in a very physically oriented society. If you ask our young students about what our basic needs are, their automatic response will be "food, shelter and clothing." As these children grow and become adults like us, they tend to focus more on what they will eat, where they will live, and what they will wear. Along with that is the remarkable obsession for a beautiful body, or anything "nice to look at." They will become caught up in the disillusion that these are what is most important and what makes them healthy. But, this is a big misconception. They will eventually come to realize that they are missing out on a lot of things, and/or are sacrificing things that are really important. Let me try to explain:

Let us look at a typical individual and understand how he can bring his integrated parts together to meet all his needs, so he can be HEALTHY and HAPPY. Here are the parts (or areas) of life, in sequence, as medical education will present them:

- PHYSICAL –your body and its desires; what you see that is obvious
- MENTAL – centered in your brain; your mind, intellect, reasoning and way of thinking.
- EMOTIONAL – your emotions or feelings; associated with the heart as the center of our emotion because of the way it is affected as it pounds when we are afraid, angry, excited or in-love.
- SPIRITUAL – your inner being, your conscience (knowing what is right and what is wrong); you cannot see, but you know it is there
- SOCIAL – those surrounding you; those you associate with and build relationships with – family, friends, etc.

- FINANCIAL – your pocket book; your checkbook balance, assets and other money matters. This is normally not included. However, I included it as I have seen the impact finances have on people.

Here is an illustration: Let's take a single young woman who finds herself attracted to a very handsome man. One day, she discovers herself battling within. Her PHYSICAL side is definitely attracted to how good-looking he is. He is very sexy and she may begin to imagine herself in his arms. Her easy-to-persuade EMOTIONS may convince her that she is "in-love" with this guy with all of her heart, mind and soul. If she is still with her senses, her more practical and MENTAL part may intercede and say, "Wait a minute! Are you crazy? How could you be attracted to, much less in-love with a guy who probably has no education, no future, and no penny to his name? You don't even have any idea where he came from." Her FINANCIAL side will interject, "If he cannot feed you, how will you feed him?" And her SPIRITUAL side may suggest, "Before you do anything, at least check his background, his character, values and beliefs. Is he married or does he have other girlfriends? Can you live with that?" Depending on what kind of friends she has, her SOCIAL side can affect her choices also. So you see how easily some girls can be carried away, while others will take the time to weigh everything first, and save themselves a lot of grief later.

Another example is on impulsive buying: The PHYSICAL side says, "I like that dress!" The EMOTIONS will immediately agree that, "It will feel wonderful to wear it." The MENTAL part will try to intercede saying, "You have so many clothes already. You don't need it." The FINANCIAL side will most likely agree. And the SPIRIT will add, "Use your money wisely." These examples are typical of what happens to us practically every minute of the day.

You see, in our physically driven society, it is so easy for anyone to like what they see, jump into it, and later realize they made a big mistake. If they had only given it some thought, it would have prevented them from unnecessary pain and regrets. The truth is, it actually takes only a few minutes of your precious time to realize that you have OTHER PARTS that need to be considered and listened to. Instead of just listening to your body or your emotions, learn to listen to your *whole-being.* Just as in a boardroom, each member has to be given a chance to share his/her views. A decision is then made according to what will best benefit everyone involved in that ONE BODY. The feet, as another example, cannot just decide to walk and jump over the bridge without recognizing that it is carrying and involving the rest of the whole body, right?

Unless all inputs are considered (as in all areas of our lives) in the decision-making process, the final result can be chaos. Blaming does not help to correct the situation. In the end, not just one or two parts suffer, but the whole person is affected and suffers the consequences. Take society, for example. It is one big planet and yet, a single man's action or a country's action, without considerations for others, has an impact on everybody involved, whether they are immediately aware of the action or the consequences.

Practical Health Tips:

- Take PREVENTIVE measures. Prevention is the best medicine. Preventive is better than curative measures. It takes less time, money, effort, pain and agony to prevent an illness or to solve a problem, than to go to the hospital and be sick in bed. Learn how to stay healthy or be totally well in the first place.
- Learn to meet the needs of each of your parts for a HEALTHY WHOLE BEING.
- Learn BALANCE and PRIORITIES for your *whole well-being.* When we take a bath, we do not just clean our face, but we bathe our whole body, right? Just like a car. Washing it is not enough. We make sure it has gas, is tuned up, has air in the tires, etc.; otherwise, it might easily break down. In the same way, we need to recognize that ALL our parts are important. You have to make the effort so that the needs of each of your six areas in life are considered and properly met to attain balanced health. The best priority in life I've heard before and I apply to my life, which I can testify to work best, is as follows:

God, first.
Family, second.
Others, third. (Could mean other people, career, business, etc.)

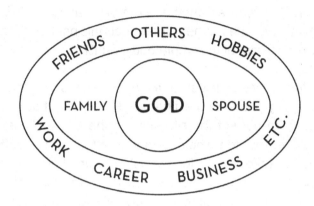

- I am an avid advocate of NATURE WALKS and/or relaxing VACATIONS. It is healthy. It gives you the break your mind, body and spirit need to rejuvenate. It is always interesting to see other places, meet and learn from different people and cultures.

- Be an INFORMED CONSUMER. There is a lot of information available in your local library or bookstore regarding total wellness and illness prevention, including being aware of natural cures vs. aggressive medical interventions; natural food supplements vs. prescribed medicines. When prescribed with a medication, treatment or procedure by your doctor, do not hesitate to *ask* him/her to explain *why* it is needed or *how* it can help you, what are the possible side effects, and are there other alternatives. As an example, keeping myself abreast with the latest health issues, I encountered a TV show that I found very interesting. Out of curiosity, I ordered the book titled, "Natural Cures" which opened my eyes to do research on some of the topics mentioned, especially regarding powerful antioxidants and other natural discoveries that boost our immune system to maintain health. And this is just one book. For your health's sake, do yourself a favor.

BE INFORMED. Because of that desire to learn, I have never been as healthy as I am now.

Health Balance and Priorities

Now that you are more familiar with the six vital areas of your being, we can then discuss how these areas can work together harmoniously as one healthy TOTAL BEING.

First, we need to know BALANCE. That means each part of our being is equally important, each has to be always considered, and each needs to be evenly met. Not one can be disregarded or ignored otherwise there will be an imbalance, which is not healthy at all. Result: an unhealthy, unfulfilled individual. Similar to a balanced diet, each basic food group is important and has to be supplied to maintain good health. When a person only takes bread and water for months, his diet is unbalanced and his dietary needs are not fully met. He may get by for a few days, but will eventually be malnourished and become sick. We do not want that to happen. We can prevent this unnecessary waste of valuable resources, our life.

These inseparable, integrated parts are assembled according to health or medically related references, just like *a team*, and presented as follows:

Physical → Mental → Emotional → Spiritual → Social
(Financial is not normally included).

To have a winning team, each player needs to be healthy, always present, and be prepared to play and win with the team. In a team, no individual is more important than the others, and no one can be disregarded. No one should be doing his own thing. A *team* is just not designed that way. Each player is aware of the different members function on the team. It is their goal to learn to work-together, as

ONE, to be a winning team. When that goal is accomplished, a great, beautiful performance and result can be expected. They play as a unified WINNING TEAM.

Just like on any team, *leadership* is equally important. That is why we have a "head coach" to direct the team, a "quarterback"' to execute a football play, a "captain or team leader" to coordinate and make sure the job gets done. Can you imagine a team with players just doing their own thing? It is just not possible for each and every member to assume the leadership role. Anyone can try, only to find out later that it does not work. It would be chaos, and eventually the team could lose the game. One person, the most qualified one, has to take the leadership role. This is where PRIORITY, or proper line-up, comes into play.

To build a winning team, a prime consideration is *WHO will take the lead*? This point is very crucial. It is vital to select the right one to take the lead in order to have a better chance of winning. "We cannot afford so many mistakes." "We cannot afford to lose" These are the statements that have been the game's guiding principle. One has to be chosen for the leading role. "We are here (to play) to WIN!" That is the goal. Could we not say and apply the same principle to our game of LIFE? Shouldn't we also treat our whole-being as "a team"?

If careful consideration is not made, with no particular goal or purpose, each of our parts will tend to do their own thing, uncoordinated and disorganized. The end result will be confusion, frustration, and in the worst cases, even mental or emotional breakdown.

Here is the mystery of life, disclosed for you and me. It is nothing new. It has been available for ages and for generations, but remains undisclosed and undiscovered by many. Those happy and victorious people I have talked about, each declared the following guiding principles as their main source, or key, for a happy, healthy, successful, victorious life. For years I have searched. Through my own personal experiences, I have tested their validity. Check them out and judge for yourself.

Can PHYSICAL effectively take the lead? We already know the answer to that. How about *mental* and *emotional*? MENTAL is more apt to directions and programming or conditioning. EMOTIONAL is reactive. Can you really imagine being lead by your emotions? It will not work. How about *social* or *financial*? Can you really allow the people or things surrounding you to direct your life? It is just not appropriate. FINANCIAL is meant to follow your state of well-being, but proven to present danger when allowed to be the lead consideration. Thus, it will not be the best one for the lead.

Here is a situation when the most assertive PHYSICAL part takes the leadership role. This is what will happen if the PHYSICAL takes the lead:

PHYSICALLY DRIVEN LIFE:

Leader's Focus: "I," "Me," and "Myself"

Other Members Role: Mental(M), Emotional(E), Spiritual(S), Social(S), Financial(F) subject to the directions and desires of the Physical.

Operational Goal: Whatever is good for the SELF at this moment, regardless of others, at any given time.

Result: A "Self-centered Life." Other members' role disregarded or suppressed. Confusion and frustration occurs. There's higher possibility of losing in the *game of life*.

Amazingly, this also explains why we have so many failures in our society. If we continue to be a stranger to one another, doing our own thing, allowing wrong choices guide us, what result can we expect?

Our society's condition, coincidentally, happens to be a reflection of what is going on with its individual members, each family and each person. It is time to do a personal check-up. Our society should focus on bringing each member on a healthy track, so we can once again have a better chance of winning - WINNING TOGETHER. When each INDIVIDUAL attains health, it results in a HEALTHIER FAMILY.

Healthier individuals and healthier families create a HEALTHY COMMUNITY and a HEALTHY SOCIETY.

Well, we cannot just wish for our world to be perfect. Let's be realistic. Most likely it will never be. But our own decision and effort is a start. Not maybe for a perfect world, but at least for a better quality of life for each of us, for all of us.

So, we are left with SPIRITUAL - the most left-out, least understood, most disregarded, and avoided. Why are we humans so stubborn and blind to see that in the first place? As if we have been blindfolded, or became too distracted to recognize the TRUTH, and to see clearly what really is good for us. This is our chance to unveil and expose the TRUTH of our SPIRITUAL side, submitted to and have a personal relationship with the Almighty God, can do(compared to a physically-driven life):

SPIRITUALLY DRIVEN LIFE

Leader's Focus: The principle of "what's RIGHT and wrong."

Other Members: M-E-P-S-F are subject to the directions and principles of the Spirit. Each member carefully considered.

Operational Goal: Whatever is for the good and benefit of self and others, taking into consideration both the present and the future.

Result: A *well-balanced, positively guided life*. Other members have harmonious relationships, working effectively together as One, resulting in a happy, healthy, successful and victorious life.

As we allow the right SPIRIT to become the driving force of our whole being, it is amazing that there is a definite command to the brain to embrace the good things, and delete or reject the bad input. This can take time, but each day is a progress. When your inputs are good and positive, the actions and outcomes are good and positive as well. No longer will the impulsive physical be the driving force, but the responsible and conscientious SPIRIT will now direct the mind and the other parts of your being. Here is the "Secret of Success" in Life formula:

SPIRIT → MIND → EMOTION → (the rest, the great outcome for the other three will follow.)

When you are mentally right, it can easily affect the emotion to act right as well. The SPIRIT, MIND and EMOTION can then automatically direct the physical to behave and take care of itself better. Then direct the financial to manage its spending money and resources wisely. If you follow this direction, do you think you will have a problem socially? Relating to and dealing with people somehow becomes no problem when you think and feel good, are considerate of others, and when you are doing your best to live your life right and well. It becomes automatic.

This is very much consistent with what God has been saying all along in His Word (The Bible): *But seek first the kingdom of God and His righteousness, and all these things shall be added to you.* (Matthew 6:33 NKJV)

ILLUSTRATION:

A. "Spiritually Driven Life" is Healthy

SPIRITUALLY HEALTHY

⇩

MENTALLY HEALTHY

⇩

EMOTIONALLY HEALTHY

⇩

PHYSICALLY HEALTHY

⇩

SOCIALLY HEALTHY

⇩

FINANCIALLY HEALTHY

B. SPIRIT AS THE CORE OF YOUR LIFE

The CORE is the SPIRIT that balances your other parts, that blends and directs your whole being.

So, let's begin your road to a better health, to total wellness or well-being, and your goal to stay in the **Healthy Zone**. This way, you will be more equipped not only to survive, but to be victorious no matter what's going on.

Spiritual Health

Know it for sure, believe it or not, you have a *spirit*. Just like your emotion, your spirit cannot be visibly seen, but you know it is there. The SPIRIT is probably the most mysterious, least understood part of our life. It is difficult to explain, and the lack of understanding of the *spirit* makes it disregarded by many.

Let's start with how *spirit* is defined, "the essence or force in man, often considered divine in origin; a part of a human being that is incorporeal and invisible and is characterized by will, self-consciousness or personality." So this is not just a matter of opinion or theory. It is a fact: each of us, including you and I, has a SPIRIT. Although it is often associated with the mind or intelligence, it should not be confused with the brain or the thought process. It is not just an emotional process either. The spirit is more than that. If the brain is like the motor of the mechanics of the car, the spirit is the very personality or nature of that car (which of course is even more complex to explain). However, it is evident that it is working closely with all the other parts of our being. Man cannot live

For generations, numerous men and women have been confused, misinformed and disillusioned about their spirituality, such that many have avoided this subject. Our world has managed to make the subject so complicated that there are people who just refuse to deal with it. We have to address this spiritual matter because our spirit, a vital part of our being, has a need that must be filled for one to attain total, healthy, well-being. If we think we can disregard or do without this spiritual side of us, we are only deceiving ourselves. We are simply exercising a denial process and therefore depriving ourselves of a basic need.

Just like a person must eat food to meet his physical needs; receive intellectual stimulation to meet his mental needs; be loved and cared for to meet his emotional needs; socialize or have meaningful relationship with others to meet his social needs; and work and get paid to meet his financial needs; likewise, he also must have a _____ to meet his spiritual need. The blank is for you to fill in and see what answer you will come up with. Go ahead. Write your answer in. Is your SPIRIT filled or it is still blank or empty?

To meet our spiritual need and enjoy spiritual health is really not that difficult or complicated at all. I will be the first to admit that I had been through all the stages of misinformation, disillusion, confusion and apathy before I found the real, simple truth. It took many years of my life to complete my discovery, but I am glad to say that I am now totally free, healthy and very happy! Once you've found the secret of the true treasures in life, you will have a deeper sense of peace and security. You will be a complete, whole-being.

Let us unveil the simple truth about our spiritual life. What can fill or meet our spiritual need? It may surprise quite a number of people to know that the answer to the blank space, to that spiritual vacuum inside us, is not a religion, nor a religious belief, nor a church affiliation, a doctrine, a fellowship, or any of those sort of things. So, there is really no such thing as to which religion, church, or religious leader is right or wrong, or better than the others when it comes to meeting our spiritual need.

While it is important for an individual, and especially for families, to go to church and learn more about God and have fellowship with fellow believers, it should be clear that it is the individual's own meaningful *personal relationship* with God that ultimately fills and meets his spiritual need. It is that simple. It is not a religion, but a *relationship*. As it is not the elaborate wedding rituals that count, but the beautiful relationship that binds the couple together that makes them a happy couple.

You cannot meet your *physical* needs by just reading a bunch of books about healthy food and a healthy body. You have to actually eat the food, exercise, rest, etc. Right? You actually have to do your part at putting those ideas into a reality. You cannot just daydream about being loved, or you'll wake up empty. It makes a huge difference when you find a real love that fills your heart. You cannot just think or imagine that you are reading all the books in the library and expect to be the smartest kid on the block. You will end up with only that – images of tons of books in the library, and nothing else.

In the same way, instead of just thinking that there must be a God or just visualizing His image, it makes a big difference when you know for sure that He is really there. It is a much more meaningful experience to know that God *is* real, in your personal life. The basic reason people do not believe in a God is because they have not experienced Him yet. It is hard for people to understand what it is like to be homeless, or relate to the joy of being in the Disneyworld, unless they have gone through the experience themselves.

If we say that God is not real and that we do not have to bother with our spiritual life, then we are only lying to ourselves. And the truth is not in us. Whether you like it or not, or are aware of it or not, each human being living on this planet has a spiritual side and need that only GOD can fill. Yes, only God can fill that void. That spiritual place in our life is reserved just for Him, and without Him, you will stay empty inside. This emptiness causes us to keep searching and wanting for more of "something." We are not even sure what is it that we are missing. Without God, we can surely fill our lives with many other gods (like money, fame, people, ideas, etc.) that eventually we will discover that these are not enough to fill our emptiness. When we use or hear the phrase, "I am missing something," think again. Is it *something* or *someone*?

Now, the question is: Is one's spirit submitted to God, or submitted to the matters of this world and its master deceiver? That explains why there are good people and there are people who do bad things. Not because some people were born bad. Have you ever seen a newborn baby who is rotten from birth? I know I have not. My long-time experience with both children and adults makes me continue to believe that each of us was created *good* for a good purpose. But then, the master deceiver and destroyer of this world, has been so effective at doing its task – to deceive, divert our attention, destroy individuals, families and relationships. We know we must fight back, but are we really a match for this powerful monster?

Why God? And why not? He is a Spirit and the very source of life, and only through having a personal relationship with Him can we have victory over the other unseen powers in this world. If we have God with us, who can be against us? Sure, you are entitled to believe it or not. What do you have to lose if you believe anyway? Will it really benefit you more if you do not believe? There will come a point when you will actually have to make that acknowledgement, make a decision whether you really want Him in your life or not. Seek within yourself and find out what you really want to be, decide what kind of life you really want to live – and is it with or without God.

I once had a meeting with two wonderful ladies in our local school association. Somehow in the course of our conversation, it got to the point where one of the ladies said she is an atheist. The other one said, "Oh, me too." They were saying that they do not believe in God nor that God existed. I had already met several other people who felt the same way so it came as no surprise to me. When I asked what made them think they are atheists, their answers focused on the disbelief of all churches and religious practices, and on what they feel are hypocrisies. As a result, they do not go to church. Since they do not go to church, they said they are atheists.

Their objections are quite valid and natural. Why are there so many religions and denominations, so many beliefs and practices? That is not even the issue. How come even supposedly religious people cannot get along? How would you answer that? I did not offer an opinion. I simply listened. Then asked, "Have you ever had a moment when something was wrong, maybe an emergency or crisis in the family, that you remembered calling on God for help?" There was a moment of silence. Then, they were both honest to say, "Yes, that's true."

It is made clear that attending a church or even being a religious person, or doing all kinds of charitable service, does not make a person right with God. We cannot buy His favor. Do you think that, when it is my turn to face God, he will actually ask me, "What is your religion or which church do you go to?" I don't think so. Even before I approach our loving God, He already knows what's in my heart – that's His only basis. (We have no use of lawyers when it comes to Him). All of us should be thankful that our merciful God is fair and just to look right into our heart and not our color, religion or church affiliation, not even at our accomplishments or level of education. God's love has no discrimination.

5 Steps to Spiritual Health:

1. **Know that GOD is REAL (Because He Is)** – Know that there is a God who truly cares about you, not only spiritually but also as a whole being.

2. **Admit that YOU NEED GOD in your life** – All you need is to believe in Him and that He is the only one who can answer all your questions and fill your every longing and need.

3. **Receive His FREE GIFT of LOVE to YOU** – All you need is to open your heart to Him, accept Him into your life, submit to His perfect plan for you (while you are still alive, He is not finished with you yet), and enjoy the experience of having a personal relationship with Him.

4. **Get to KNOW GOD BETTER** – The more you know about Him and how special you really are to Him, the more you can enjoy your fellowship with Him.

5. **Walk with Him daily** – In His Word He says, "I will never leave you nor forsake you." Believe it! He is there for you twenty-four hours a day, seven days a week, rain or shine. Awake or asleep. (If someone tells you otherwise, ask if that someone can do the same for you.)

If you are serious about your desire to know more about God, want answers to any questions you may have, clear some doubts (if there are any), I only know of one authorized and reliable book that I can recommend. Some call it "The Holy Book,"' some call it "The Bible" or "God's Word." I like to call it "The BOOK OF LIFE." It is also the number one recommended guide by many highly successful, respected and happy individuals who found God as their true treasure. If you feel that great people like Abraham Lincoln, Martin Luther King Jr., Billy Graham, Mother Teresa and so many other wise and accomplished people, they acknowledge this Book as their source of true knowledge and understanding. As this book says, "... man shall not live by bread alone; but by every word that proceeds from the mouth of the Lord."

The *Book of Life* has been the best-seller of all times since 1611, the only book translated into hundreds of languages and dialects, and the only book being distributed to every corner of the world. It is being read and treasured by people of all walks of life - rich and poor, scholars, professors, engineers, scientists, and the famous and simple everyday people.

This Book is truly amazing. It is a complete library by itself, that covers all subjects you could ever think of: Love, Marriage, Divorce, Child-rearing, Family, Law, Medicine, Business Management, Success, Finance, Debt, Taxes, History, Math, etc. It includes our past, present and future, and especially LIFE and how to live it. It was relevant and applicable four centuries ago, and still is today.

By the way, I find it interesting that the very first schools, which did not have the supplies of books we have now, used this Book as their textbook. If you only read one book in your lifetime, this is it. It is worth every minute you spend reading it. You will get to know God better and find the answers to your questions. In it you will find life, YOUR LIFE, as well.

Our true God is faithful and you can always count on Him. You will no longer feel alone, hopeless or helpless anymore. You will find worrying as an obsolete subject. That surely will make you happy, and that is healthy!

Have you filled in the BLANK yet?

Mental Health

Are you fascinated with modern technology? The age of computers, network satellites, superhighways, etc.? Those amazing gadgets devices and machines, which, we should be reminded, are all created by man himself. If these fascinate you, you should be more amazed with the BRAINS that created them! Yet, it is unfortunate that until now, with all these wonderful things, mankind remains to have a very limited understanding of how this amazing brain, this living computer actually functions. All we know is that we have the ability to think and do great things.

Our brain works pretty much like a computer. In fact, a computer is designed to think and function like the most intelligent brain there is. The brain is designed for you to think, and respond to your very thoughts and directions. When you say or think "sad", the message is relayed to your brain and through its complex processing, causes your facial muscles to droop down (you look down and out), and may even cause you to have teary eyes. When you say or think "happy", the brain processing causes your facial muscles to feel upbeat and energetic, and a smile automatically radiates from your beautiful face. When you say "I will do it", the message is again relayed, and amazingly your actions are directed towards doing what you said you would do. When you say, "I don't like to do that," then your body does as directed – it does nothing until you change its direction.

Actually, whenever we are confronted with a situation, the brain simply translates that to us; then waits for our response, of what we want to do next. Basically, we make a choice: love or hate, fight or flight, attack or forgive, do something or do nothing, etc. Those who create advertising understand this process very well. And it works, doesn't it? They call this "human psychology"; give a stimulus in such a way that it creates a desirable response.

It is very reassuring to know that within each of us are amazing natural abilities, commonly called inborn impulses, instincts, and reflexes. These automatically help or protect us at times when there is no time to even think. Take time to get to know yourself better, that way the more you can trust your abilities and your natural instincts to make the right choices.

Going back to our powerful brain, remember the computer rule: Garbage in, garbage out. MENTAL HEALTH means putting the right input into our brain to produce the right results or output. Think of good things and good things will eventually happen. Feed your brain with good information and produce more productive and satisfying results.

With continuous practice, you will also discover the magic and the wisdom of learning how to turn negatives into POSITIVES. Be constantly aware of it until you develop the habit. When you begin to feel bad or negative, focusing on the negatives does not help the situation. Find a reason to count your blessings instead. Think about what you can learn from the situation. Focus on positive, beautiful things. You will have a better chance of getting good, positive results and being successful in life.

Here are some practical tips for MENTAL HEALTH:

READ. READ. READ. – There is so much to learn. Do not waste your time with junk, useless reading, or just sitting in front of the television. Use your time wisely by reading informative books, like *how-to* books or topics that will be useful in your everyday life. Read about real people, great people and their accomplishments, inspiring stories, or practical ideas for living a better life. With internet access, you can research and access more relevant and vital information. Equip yourself with good knowledge.

- **LISTEN. LISTEN. LISTEN.** – We share or give to others when we are talking. If you wish to benefit more, learn to listen and receive. You can learn something from everyone, experts and everyday people. It is amazing how much you can learn from other people's experiences. Their treasures will become your treasures, too.

- **RETAIN GOOD INPUT.** – Reject and discard bad inputs and thoughts. You can learn to do this, just like a computer can delete and reprogram.

- **EXERCISE YOUR BRAIN.** – You will be amazed at its capacity and capabilities. Use your imagination to draw a picture. Write about something. Figure out a problem. Experiment with your ideas. Maybe even come up with another great invention, or a fantastic idea to help solve some of mankind's problems. Do not limit yourself. I have learned that humans use only 10% or less of their brain capacity. If that is true, then that is such a waste. On a positive note, can you imagine how much more can possibly be accomplished with the rest of our capacity?

I am sure you have heard the phrase, "The sky is the limit!" So, what are you waiting for? Go on, search, research, imagine, discover, create, accomplish something, share and make a contribution. Yes, life is much better than you may think. Be thankful for your wonderful gift. Utilize it well so that you may find more satisfaction and meaning in life through gracefully sharing it with others.

So, do you feel young or old? It is not really a matter of age, you know. Are you happy, sad, poor, or rich? Interestingly, the answer is simply a state of mind.

Emotional Health

Do you feel emotional sometimes? No problem. You are human, and we humans have emotions. What exactly is emotion? The dictionary defines it as "a strong surge of feeling marked by an impulse to outward expression, often accompanied by complex bodily reaction." We cannot visibly see it, but we know it is there. We feel it. Haven't you heard or said to someone, "I can see you are sad"; "My, you are happy today!" "It looks like someone is in-love." How did you or they know? Emotions are any strong feeling like love, hate, anger, fear, joy, etc., often translated through bodily action. We don't carry signs with us to announce how we feel, but it is interesting that whatever we feel is well reflected and perceived by others. This is called "body language." Is what you are saying consistent to what you are showing? Be aware, it shows.

It is very important that we become aware of the way we feel. We have to remind ourselves that we have other parts which we have to consider, and do a constant balance check with. Just like the physical aspect of our being, our *emotions* tend to be very impulsive. Say a young girl meets a good-looking guy at a party. Just because she felt something unusual or a "chemistry" going on, that does not mean she is already "in love."' It is time to think! And it is always wise for her to take a moment to consult with her other integrated parts, or she could possibly do something drastic she may regret later. Checking, thinking about it, and reasoning within oneself can save people a lot of pain and agony later.

Going back to our young girl. If she just follows her sudden surge of feeling saying, "This must be love," and impulsively goes with the guy, she'll forget to even check out who he really is, where he came from, etc., as if those don't matter. She does not realize that it could be, and most likely it is, a mere lust or a strong physical attraction. As soon as the physical desire is satisfied or gone, she will likely feel sadness and regret.

Often, it is too late to find out much needed information to avoid the undesirable results of an action. Thinking that it was for the sake of experimentation or adventure does not seem to relieve the pain either. This happens a lot among teens, resulting in early or unwanted pregnancies. Those who resorted to abortion, thinking it is an easy way out, then live with the guilt and regret for a long time. Those who did not mean to be unfaithful to their spouses, end up having a lengthy and painful divorce. Those who never thought about the consequences of a single, fleeting moment, could find themselves agonizing over a disease they may have contacted. Those few moments could, and have, led to broken relationships, problems affecting jobs and careers, personal finances, even destroying reputations beyond repair. In some situations, the chain of events lead from one to another, resulting in various addictions, nervous breakdowns, and even suicide.

It sounds ugly, yet we hear of this practically every day. From one simple, seemingly harmless wholesome feeling, to a very unpleasant ending. Who would have even thought of the result? All because of not taking a moment to pause, to think, to check. Other situations result from uncontrolled anger and hate. We hear lots of stories on TV news and in the newspapers involving horrible violent crimes, including domestic violence. Who is to blame? People tend to point fingers at each other. That is the usual impulse, as if blaming someone or something else could reverse the situation. Blaming does not help. Each of us has to take responsibility for our actions, to be in control of our emotions. Do a check and balance before doing anything, weighing the circumstance and the pros and cons.

Concentrate on absorbing and sharing more constructive emotions like LOVE and JOY. Be aware that emotions such as hate, fear, or depression, do not do you, or anyone else any good. Fear can be deadly. Later, we will talk about dealing with fear of the unknown.

Depression is becoming a very serious problem among all ages, from young children to seniors. Depression is a state of excessive sadness or hopelessness, usually with accompanying physical symptoms, associated with loneliness or feeling alone, unworthiness, grief, or finding no hope, no purpose or no meaning in life. Lighten up. It is normal for us humans to feel that way every now and then.

The weather, our hormones and certain situations that we deal with every day affect us. Again, you are not alone! Millions of other people around you could be depressed when faced with a mounting pile of bills. It is not the end of the world for you.

The best way to deal with this type of emotion is to divert your attention to something else, like other people or nature. Since I have had plenty of those moments, I can share with you some ideas that have helped me. I do meet or see people around who I found out have sadder circumstance than what I have - someone with dirty clothes, maybe not even a home. One day I saw a couple digging in a huge trash bin. Another time, I saw a person with no legs, on a wheelchair crossing the street, or a blind man with his dog, a sick lady with all those life-extending gadgets at a hospital unit. As I think about them, I feel I have many more reason to be thankful for. As I pray for those people, I feel energy to get up and do more worthwhile things than just sit or lie there feeling depressed, doing nothing. Sometimes, I go out, go for a walk, look at the trees and their beautiful leaves, hear the birds, or whatever beautiful and positive things that can fill my mind.

Remember that while there are people crying, there are people celebrating. While there are people dying, new babies are being born. If you feel depressed, give yourself physical and mental rest; it will help your emotions heal as well. When your brain gets rest, it will be more relaxed and can function better. Going through depressing moments ourselves, helps us relate better with others.

Yes, emotions can be mastered and controlled. Who said you cannot have emotions? Emotions can be so beautiful and wonderful when they can lead to something good and useful. Like "true love," It can be the most wonderful thing a person can share with someone who mutually loves the other person.

Physical Health

To be physically healthy, the following are very important:

1. **NUTRITIOUS FOOD** – Learn moderation and variety with each meal and snack. Have equal portions of PROTEINS, the body building food (meats, poultry, seafood, nuts, beans, etc.); CARBOHYDRATES, the energy giving food (rice, cereal, potato, bread, etc.); VITAMINS and MINERAL SOURCES, the body and immune system boosters, or disease and illness prevention food (mainly vegetables and fruits).

   Eat more fresh fruits and vegetables. The more fresh and natural the food, the more nutrients you can get. Try to stay away from processed food which has little or no nutrients, but only extra calories that can give you unnecessary extra pounds, especially the following: white sugar, salt, bleached flour. If at all possible, use honey, sea salt and whole grains instead. Food supplements in a more natural form is better than chemically based.

   How much food? That depends on your build, activities and health conditions. Learn to listen to your body. It will tell you. Do not let your emotions dictate the amount that you should eat. Be as consistent as possible. It is not good to skip meals.

   NOTE: If time allows, if your doctor tells you that you have some sort of terminal illness, don't panic. You may want to consider a second opinion, and/or alternative remedies. It could be as simple as a nutritional approach, which has already helped many people. It is more comfortable than invasive approaches. You have to be agreeable and comfortable with your decision and the medical professionals you will work with to help you win the battle before you allow anything done to you. You are entitled to that.

2. **WATER** – Clean, fresh water is necessary for proper body functions. It helps facilitate the nourishment of our body cells and the elimination of body wastes and toxins. About 6-8 glasses a day is desirable. Drink water regularly without having to wait until you feel thirsty. Most of the food we eat naturally contains water. Juice and milk are not substitutes for water, but better than soda or colored drinks. If you are concerned about the quality of the water you are drinking (depending on where you live or in the event of a natural calamity), have it tested, or boil your drinking water as necessary.

3. **EXERCISE** – Children are naturally active. If not, encourage them to start right now. For us adults, regular exercise (as allowable) is recommended. We vary with our work nature and activities, so learn to listen to your body and what it needs or how much it can take. Walk or be on your feet more than sitting, BE ACTIVE! This is wonderful for your health as it improves your circulation and activates your metabolism to burn the calories you've put on. It also helps build your muscles, which naturally burn more calories. Too much exercise can be as bad as too little or nothing at all. Brisk walking, jogging, jumping rope, dancing or swimming will do well. One does not have to own exercise equipment or belong to a gym to exercise and stay fit. If you can afford it, and think it will help motivate you more then go for it. Exercise helps you look your best and feel good about yourself, which in turn helps make you happy and contributes to your overall success.

4. **BATH or PERSONAL HYGIENE** – After a long, tiring day or waking up in the morning to go to work, nothing refreshes us better than a good bath or shower! There is just something magical about it – like a plant under the rain or a car after a car wash. It cleanses and refreshes us – we look, smell and feel good! Even the motion of bathing provides a simple exercise that improves our circulation. It helps us prevent skin diseases as well.

5. **REST and RELAXATION** – Take plenty of R&R. This does not mean being lazy, but when you are working hard, long hours, and you are beginning to feel some discomfort, sleepy, burned out, stressed out, it is your body telling you "Take a break!" Learn to listen to your body. Like a moving car, when the sign says STOP, you better stop or else. When the gas gauge says empty, you better fill it up. If you want you and your body to get along, to function well and together avoid problems, then do as it suggests. Sleeping 6-8 hours per day is recommended. When you are driving or working and you feel sleepy or unable to concentrate, stop. Pull over if you are driving or shut your eyes if you are working and give yourself a few minutes to rest. Listening to soothing music, singing, watching children, taking a walk, or simple breathing exercises are other ways to help you to become calm, relaxed and rested.

6. **SHELTER and CLOTHING** – Whoever came up with the idea that food, shelter and clothing are our three basic needs was only thinking of our physical needs. We are now finding that those are not the only physical needs we have and definitely NOT our whole-being's ONLY needs. Amazingly, most schools continue to teach those three basic needs to our children. Food, I absolutely agree with. Yes, decent, comfortable shelter and clothing are important to have, but let's face it, we will not just die for lack of them. Today, we have a lot of homeless people who have neither a decent place to live nor decent clothes to wear, yet amazing, are surviving. Clean, comfortable shelter and clothing are desirable and necessary to provide us warmth and privacy. But to put so much importance on them, to the point of being buried in debt to have a fancy home, or closets of dresses (which we may not even wear), becomes a big problem instead.

You need to distinguish basic needs from extravagance, excess and just plain unnecessary. If you need or really want it, and you can afford it, do not deprive yourself. Go for it! Treat yourself sometimes, without guilt. If you have some extras, you may find it very gratifying to share them with others less fortunate.

NOTE: A lot of times our *physical* side needs to be tamed. Both our *physical* and *emotional* sides are more concerned with the present desires and feelings. What's important to these two is *now.* Learn to recognize that and be quick to balance it with the other parts of your *whole being.*

> *It's bizarre that the produce manager is more important to my children's health than the pediatrician.* - Meryl Streep, American Actor

> *Look to your health; and if you have it, praise God, and value it next to a good conscience; for health is the second blessing that we mortals are capable of; a blessing that money cannot buy.* - Izaak Walton

> *The patient should be made to understand that he or she must take charge of his own life. Don't take your body to the doctor as if he were a repair shop.* -Quentin Regestein

Social Health

To be socially healthy is not difficult at all when you feel good, have the right attitude, have respect and consideration for others, etc. There is no need to struggle with trying to please everybody – you can never please everybody. Just be yourself. It will come. The more you understand your SELF, the more you will understand OTHERS, and better relate with them. Furthermore, to be socially adaptive and happy, remember the following:

- **We are all UNIQUE INDIVIDUALS** – We are all different from each other. As previously discussed, no two individuals in this world are exactly alike, in appearance, way of thinking, mood or feelings, lifestyle, likes and dislikes, beliefs and opinions, etc. Not even identical twins born and raised together. Each of us is very SPECIAL. So do not expect others to think the same way you do and don't be irritated if others do it differently or have different opinion. Learn to respect others' individualities so they respect yours as well.
- **We are all created equal** – At first you may disagree. You may say, "How come there are those who are rich and those who are poor. Some are short, some are tall; some are pretty, some are not very pretty; some are black, brown, white, etc.?" Yes, that is true. That is all part of us being different and unique individuals. But in many ways we are the same and are created equal, and no one should feel left out or disadvantaged. Each of us has the opportunity to excel, to be the best that we can be in spite of our imperfections. Opportunities may vary, but are equally available for all of us.

Somehow, we become more focused on how we are different, rather than our similarities. We all have the same basic needs. None of us can live without food, water and oxygen. We are balanced and equal in a way that no matter what your sex, color, education or socioeconomic background, each person has a problem or some imperfection in his or her life. This includes the royalty, the rich and famous, who supposedly, have everything! Maybe some of them even envy an ordinary person's freedom and privacy. Having so much wealth can actually become a burden or a big challenge to many of them. They cannot go around freely because they are always concerned about their safety. So which life do you want to have? Amazingly, you will always find two people on each end of the rope wanting to switch ends with each other.

- **Put yourself in someone's shoes** – "Do to others what you want others to do to you." How would you feel, think, react, if you were in their position. Understand instead of criticizing or judging. Don't be so quick to take things personally when a person around you seems to be angry or ignoring you. It is possible that the person has a personal problem that is affecting him that may have nothing to do with you at all.

- **Do not take your loved ones for granted** – Life is too short. Express your love, in words and in deeds while you can. Spending time with your love ones is the best expression of love and care you can give. Don't wait to do a good deed tomorrow. Do it now.

- **Life is a give and take process** – The more you learn to be a GIVER, the more will come back to you. Give your love, your time, talent or whatever else you can share. It is your best investment. You cannot lose and you will be happy with its return. Learn to be a gracious receiver also, for you will then have more to give.

- **We are ALL in this Earth TOGETHER** – Whether we like it or not, we affect each other, negatively or positively, healthy or unhealthy. Be angry or be happy and watch how the people around you react. It is highly contagious! So, spread more good tidings to our environment. Be happy! Be positive. It is good for ALL of us.

(Note: Insert "Circle of Life" here – You at the center-> Earth

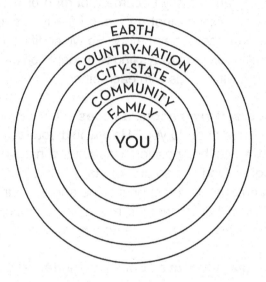

Financial Health

Financial matters and money have always been a major part of our everyday life. Some do it well, some do not. Nobody likes to be financially unstable, but can happen to anybody. I have found out that financial education is very important to young children as soon as they start to receive money and begin learning how to spend it. The following tips, as a start, could contribute to an individual's financial health:

It takes SELF-DISCIPLINE not to spend what you do not have. It is wiser to wait a little bit to save the money you need to buy what you need instead of 'charging' it now. And then suffer a long time realizing you are paying about twice as much due to the interest. No matter how good the advertising, STAY AWAY from using credit cards! Experience should teach you that the plastics should be used only for its original purpose, *identification* and *emergency use only.* Discard the word "convenient," it is certainly not.

When you pay by cash, it helps control your spending since you cannot buy what you do not have the money for. At least, you will go home with no headache or worry about paying for it later. It is so easy to charge everything that it can get out of hand. The result, in most cases, is very ugly. Usually follows are nasty, humiliating collections, bankruptcy, foreclosure, even divorces and suicide. I am seeing the reality of this phrase I heard before, "The borrowers become slaves to the lenders." Have you heard of the other AIDS that is deadlier than the actual disease itself? This one has already affected close to 90% of our nation's population. The Acquired INCOME DEFICIENCY Syndrome (another AIDS) has been sweeping the nation at a very alarming rate. Wake up! Know what we are dealing with here. The first thing you can do if you are affected is to learn to live within your means. Before buying anything, try to answer these questions first:

1. Do I NEED it?
2. Can I AFFORD it? Or, can it WAIT?
3. Is it TAX deductible?
4. Is it GOOD for me long term? Will it GROW?

If you honestly answer YES to at least three of these questions, then you cannot go wrong. If not, or if you have any doubts, take the necessary caution. Am I making an issue about 'buying'? I guess I am, because this is when we stumble the most, don't we? Yes, we want to help move our economy by spending, but when people now suffer because of spending by credit or with money that they don't have in the first place, even our government, our society will suffer at the end. People need to wake up to the reality that even our special, memorable holidays became too commercialized. Have you not notice yet that we just have too many occasions to celebrate now? Do we really have to be in debt just for decors and costumes? Isn't this all about 'BUSINESS' and merchants making money? Do we really still experience the true meanings of the occasions when we are financially burdened? Isn't just being with the people we love or care about, even with just simple dinner get-together, more than sufficient? Sure each one has the choice to continue with the trap of financial bondage, or start fresh evaluating what has true meaning and value to what we do.

Learn to BUDGET. It is simpler than you think.

I have to admit that I really did not learn about this until age twenty-two, when I started receiving paycheck, or I can call real income. Prior to that, I really did not have any money to budget. I sometimes wonder if they even taught budgeting in school. Nevertheless, I started to learn, which was fun at first, especially when I had more income than expenses. Then I got married and had three children. Life got more complicated. I then began to learn more about *negative balance, deficit,* and the need for a *'strict budget.'*

Let me share with you some techniques I learned from the experts coupled with my own experiences. As a starter, regardless of your age or financial situation, you can do SIMPLE BUDGETING:

First, get a pad or a notebook; draw a vertical line down the middle (or fold it in half). Next, write on the left 'INCOME," or what is coming in on a monthly basis from all resources. If it varies, figure out the most reasonable average amount, or use the lowest figure to be safe.

Then, write 'EXPENSES' on your right. Below that, write down all your expenses, including but not limited to: basic necessities according to priorities like house payment, food/grocery, insurances, utilities, car payment & gas, etc. Write down the actual or most realistic figures you can – check your receipts, checkbook, charge account, etc. Evaluate and differentiate the needs/necessities vs. extras/wants. Note that your expenses should not exceed your income. They should either balance or, ideally, your income should always exceed your expenses (even a little), so you have something to set aside for SAVINGS (planned vacation, things to buy, repair and maintenance, etc.), for EMERGENCY FUND (important for any unforeseen needs, like medical problem, lay-off, etc., and for INVESTMENTS (retirement, children's college, etc.). At least three months emergency income is recommended by the experts. More, if it is possible. PLANNING is very important. Small, gradual savings or investment is definitely much better than nothing.

If your expenses are higher, be alarmed. That is a warning sign that you are not financially well. Unlike a fever, this one does not go away by itself. You have to do something to get back on track or you will be in more trouble later. Evaluate your expenses and see which ones you can cut or eliminate. You may wish to stick more with water for a while than colored drinks. After all, plain water is healthier. Do you really have to have that many channels on your TV? Do you even have time to watch all the channels; better question is how much productive time you (and the children) spend or waste in front of the tube? Do you have to shop for more clothes that most likely will just crowd your closet or buy more things that just stock up in the garage? I was once, twice guilty of these, that's how I know. Keep finding alternatives, ways and means to save. Some people are financially wiser and getting ahead, more secure and worry-less, while a lot of us are more naïve and have to learn the hard way. We hope that our future generations will be wiser.

When you have a balanced budget, you do not have to worry about the pressure of having another job. You would not need anything beyond your eight hours of work so you can still enjoy your life. You did not come into this world just to work 12-16 hours or more a day just to pay your bills or worry about your bills, did you? Your BUDGET SHEET is one of your most important assignments for life, so keep up with it.

My Financial Picture (Simple Budget Example)

Income (per month)	Expenses (per month)	
Take home pay: $3,500.	Giving (you decide):	$400.
	Savings/Emergency:	$400.
	Residence:	$1,000.
	Groceries:	$800.
	Auto Expenses:	$500.
Other Sources: $ 500.	Insurances:	$200.
	Utilities:	$250.
	Credit (if any):	$50.
	Misc. (Invest/ Retirement):	$400.
TOTAL: $4,000.	TOTAL:	$4,000.

Note: This is only an example. The actual one you will create will be based on your situation. This is to bring realization of your current financial picture so you can be more aware of the areas to improve.

Remember this saying, "It is not how much money you make that counts, it is what you keep." The savings and emergency section under EXPENSES are for the saying, "Pay yourself first (if you can)." There is actually a lot more to learn about this particular subject, like assets and liabilities to determine your NET WORTH. Want to see yours? It's simple: Total assets (worth of what you own) minus total liabilities (you owe) = net worth. How is yours?

Other important things to consider:

- **Live within your means.** Stay out of debt as much as possible, as soon as possible. Develop the discipline to maintain only one to two credit cards for the purpose of ID (identification) and extreme emergency only. You probably have already heard, there are two types of debt: good credit and bad credit. Learn the difference. Learn to use the good one, and stay away from the bad one that can enslave you and keep you in poverty

- **Set your priorities, always remembering the giving principle.** Set aside at least the first 10% to cheerfully give as your seed, to your church and/or other worthy cause that you believe in. The giving principle works! *The more you give, the more you receive.*

- **Pay yourself first** before all the bills, to save or invest on systematic, periodic means, like an IRA plan. Others consider real estate, gold or precious metals and stones as great investments. Always consider and update your emergency funds, insurances (life, health, long-term care or retirement, auto – in that order). Learn yourself or consult someone you can trust about any investment, land banking, self-directed retirement plans, etc. to help you on these areas before making a move.

Learning to manage what you have is the trick of the financial game. Many of those who have won the lotto, received an inheritance, made millions on movies, in sports, in business, etc. lost when they spent their money carelessly or trusted the wrong person to handle their finances. A lot of them ended up broke. It is equally interesting that there are people who have learned to live a simple, worry–free life, feeling rich and secure, even with little income, just because they know how to manage what they have wisely… and that is healthy.

"I think everybody should get rich and famous and do everything they ever dreamed of so they can see that it's not the answer."
– Jim Carrey, American Actor

"What can be added to the happiness of a man who is in health, out of debt, and has a clear conscience?"
– Adam Smith, Economist & Philosopher

Chapter 3

Yes, You Can Survive Tough Times

Beyond the clouds, there is the blue sky.
After the rain, there is sunshine.
Tough times don't last and
naturally disappear in time.

*A*fter reading all the information I have shared with you from the previous chapter, you may wonder why I still had to go through some difficult times. I will remind you that at that time I only knew about half of this valuable information. The remaining half most I learned the hard way. Lessons I appreciated only *after* experiencing those tough times. That confirms what I used to hear from some of my former teachers, *"Experience is still the best teacher"* and *"Practice is the best trainer."*

"Life is... not a bed of roses." There are times in your life when you have wonderful, beautiful moments. Moments like holding a beautiful rose, exploring its petals, admiring the radiant colors, and enjoying its sweet fragrance. Moments that make you forget about the rest of the world for a while and all you know is you just want to linger and hold on to those precious moments.

But suddenly, like waking up from a daydream, you feel a sharp pain as a thorn pricks your finger. You forgot about the thorns. Isn't it interesting that the more beautiful the rose is, the bigger the thorns? You wonder. Do roses really have to come with thorns?

That's how life is. Life surely is beautiful. But along with its beauty are painful, trying moments we refer to as *tough times*, also referred to as *challenges, tests, trials, tribulations, ordeals,* etc. I personally have been through many, some I admit were too difficult to bear that I felt like giving up.

In this section, you will see how everything we have talked about in the previous chapters applies. The decision to make my life and my family's life an open book is for you to know that these situations are real. They do happen. You may be able to relate with some, or remind you of someone you know who is going through a similar situation. Whatever the circumstance, no one is absolutely alone in his or her ordeal. The most important message is to know that THERE IS ALWAYS HOPE. Behind those clouds are blue skies. After the rain, there is bright, beautiful sunshine. After the cold winter snow that leaves the trees and grounds barren and seemed lifeless, spring comes with a new beginning, fresh green grass, new leaves on trees, and beautiful flowers once again. After the dark, stormy night comes a new day ... a new beginning.

Mistakes and Failures are Stepping Stones

"Those things that hurt instruct."
– Benjamin Franklin

Do you know of anyone who has not made a mistake? Nobody. In one way or another, each one of us has made mistakes and is likely to make some more. A mistake is an error in action, judgment, perception, or understanding. It is a natural part of our life, a part of the learning process. It serves a purpose, especially for those of us who learn better the hard way.

This should not make us feel down like a total failure. And quit. If we look at each mistake and failure more positively and learn the lesson from them, in the end we will see these as great necessities that help us grow and mature to become a better person. That is what hands-on and learning from experience is all about.

We always hear that "Everybody makes mistakes." That is true and no one is exempt. So why do we feel so down on ourselves when we are obviously not alone in this situation? Is it not simply because of our feeling of embarrassment, or fear of humiliation or rejection that we even try to hide it? Of course, it hurts. It can be very painful and demeaning at times. But what is it there to be ashamed about?

When I was a child, my father used to tell us, "There is nothing to be ashamed about poverty and honest mistakes. The only time you should be ashamed is when you did something wrong." These words, first of all, gave me some clarification of the term. A 'mistake' is unintentional. After all, who would be crazy enough to do something that you already know is not right and will not work or will only result in disaster? Well, some people still do. That is not a mistake. That is a willful wrongdoing, for whatever purpose and result they are trying to accomplish. They cannot escape from the natural cause and effect rule though. Sooner or later, whatever is sown, that will be reaped also. It never fails.

So, you wonder why people continue to do wrong. Don't they know the clear path warning? Should we include this in our invisible life path manual? WARNING: "Wrongdoing is an offense with corresponding severe penalties. Any violator will not go unpunished." An offender may manage to get away from the court, but our nature has its own way of making sure that justice is done. Whether you like it or not, that is the truth. Accept it or not, that is the way our life on earth operates.

We can prevent wrongdoing. We have a free will to choose to do right or to do wrong. It is up to us to make a decision and make a choice. We are very capable of doing what we choose or decide to do, once we put our mind to it.

Since a mistake is unintentional and we have no prior knowledge of what the outcome will be, it is difficult to avoid mistakes as we subject ourselves to daily trials and errors. You are actually taking a chance. You are in the process of learning to find out later if your theory or your gut feeling is right or wrong. So, do not be afraid of your mistakes. On the other hand, you can take some precautions and try to prevent any unnecessary mistakes. Reading, researching and simply asking questions first to verify and increase your knowledge on the subject matter can be very important preventive measures, and are valuable tools to the learning process.

FAILURES? Same thing. In fact, come to think of it, there is really no such thing as failure. It is just a negative connotation created by those people who have little understanding and yet love to condemn and put down people's shortcomings. Why be bothered by them? They are surely no help anyway. Sure we make mistakes. Some people consider that a failure, that is why they sometimes quit. But if we stop focusing on the mistake or failure, learn from it and move ahead, then we can do better next time, and we will finally succeed, grow and develop into a better more mature person.

Wise people say, "Mistakes and failures can either break you or mold you." That is true, but I prefer to say that it should not even break you at all. So, the only time we actually fail is when we quit or give up. Do not give up. There are still a lot of great chances, better opportunities and bright days ahead of you. Every day you wake up is a new beginning. There are still plenty of doors for you to open.

How do I know? Of course, I am already an expert. I already committed so many mistakes and, as people call it, "failed" so many times. After all that I have been through, it is truly a miracle I am still up, alive and excited about life.

Most importantly, you can survive these mistakes and failures too.

> *"Some of the best lessons we ever learn, we learn from our mistakes and failures. The error of the past is the success and wisdom of the future."*
> – Tyron Edwards, American Theologian

Problems Can Be Better Dealt With

> *"If there was nothing wrong in the world, there wouldn't be anything for us to do."*
> – George Bernard Shaw, Irish Essayist

Yes, there is a better way for you and I to handle problems, instead of the problems handling you, or us.

Do you have problems? Of course, who does not have one?

We always hear that "nobody is perfect." In fact, nobody's life is perfect. So what then is the point of feeling sorry for yourself when you are not alone? Everyone has their own problems, maybe even worse than yours. Out of all the people you know, how many know your problem? One? Two? Nobody? So everybody else is thinking,

"Lucky you, you are perfectly fine, you have no problems." They just don't know. And you are probably thinking the same thing about those around you, which is why you are thinking that you are the only one who has such a huge problem. Just like mistakes, nobody wants to talk about them; we do not announce our problems to the world. What is the real problem here?

The problem is... the word is so misused of overused that we think of problem as something dreadful. Just hearing or thinking of the word makes some people perceive it as a disaster. The word has gained such a bad reputation we seem to misuse it on just about everything and every situation we encounter - problem with the weather, cars, traffic, work, school, kids, pets, money, etc. It is insane! Have we forgotten our school days when the word problem was used interchangeably with words such as hypothesis, question, or situation, meaning, we are confronted with a perplexing or puzzling question, idea or situation that just needs to be studied or analyzed to derive a more concrete answer or solution. That is no big deal. It is positive. That is where the challenge comes from, a part of our life process.

Another issue is, we linger too much on the perceived problems that get us down. Why not FOCUS on the SOLUTIONS and ways to resolve things or improve the situation instead.

Situations come to us every day to keep us from getting bored and to get us into doing something meaningful and productive. These situations will never go away as long as we live. So why not take them as welcome partners in life? Why not look at or call problems as SITUATIONS, QUESTIONS or IDEAS whichever is more applicable. That may help change our view or prospective and deal with these problems better. Another way is, instead of being in the box totally involved with the situation, it may help to look at situations from outside the box to see things more objectively.

I remember a friend who spoke at a seminar in Miami, Florida, who said to the audience, "Problems will always be there. But you know what? If your attitude is right, YOU GOT NO PROBLEM!" What problem?

The Problem-Solving Process

I actually learned this problem-solving process when I was a nursing student. I am pretty sure that other courses or professions have a similar version, too. As professional nurses, we apply this process to our Patient Care Plans when we approach a problem we have identified with our patients and clients. It is a very important and helpful tool that the health team uses everyday at the hospital, clinic, or in the field.

Little did I know that I could also use it in my everyday life, not only at work, but at home, in my marriage, for raising our children, but also in dealing with other people and various situations. It is practical and very helpful as it taught me to slow down and look into the situation first before I jump to any conclusion or commit to any drastic action. It has become so valuable to me and my family that I thought I would share it with you.

FIVE STEPS IN PROBLEM SOLVING:

1. IDENTIFY the Problem (or Situation) – Be specific.

2. ANALYZE the Problem – Assess or examine the underlying factors or circumstances that may be contributing to the problem.

3. FORMULATE a PLAN of ACTION – Make a goal or objective to cure or resolve the identified problem. List down specific actions toward accomplishing that goal.

4. IMPLEMENT – Do it! Do or act as planned to possibly solve the problem and expect a good result.

5. EVALUATE – Assess the effectiveness of the Action Plan and Intervention. If it is effective, good for you! If not, start the process again; try other possibilities and alternatives for solutions. Included here are considerations for preventive measures, to avoid the reoccurrence of the same problem.

Example:

A. **PROBLEM**: Losing a job. Yes, you just learned you are now "jobless". (I can share this with you since my husband and I have personally experienced this kind of situation, not once but several times).

B. **ANALYSIS**:

1. There must be a reason why you were laid off (or worse, unreasonably "fired"). If you were laid off, consider that the company may have no other choice, i.e., they could be losing money or on the verge of closing their business unless they do something. If you were fired, be reasonable. There may be something to learn from it or something to be thankful for eventually.

2. The effect on you (and your family) of not having a paycheck: not being able to pay the bills nor buy other basic necessities. You're seeing the disaster! But, if you look further, you may discover that there is actually a light at the end of the tunnel. Don't rush into conclusions or drastic actions that you may regret later. Just about everyone experiences trying events like this, yet survived and did even better afterward. You are not alone and there is always hope, a solution and a brighter tomorrow.

C. **PLAN OF ACTION**:

1. Take into consideration your company's condition, why they have to lay-off people. They may not want to lay-off anybody but the business is maybe going through tough times. Don't take it personally. They have to do what they have to do. If you were to find a better and higher paying job, you would probably not hesitate to say goodbye also. If you were fired, either that company does not deserve you, or there may be a lesson that you can learn from. When one door closes, a better one opens. Find another perfect match that can better

appreciate your talents and contributions. Make plans for survival in the meantime while you are looking for another job.

2. Again, the name of the game is SURVIVE! The game of survival directs us to do whatever it takes in order to survive in a more constructive way. (Helpful tips can be found throughout this book) It may be difficult for a while, but if you remain up, continue moving, looking, persevering and praying, eventually the tough times will pass.

D. **IMPLEMENTATION**:

1. Get up and get out! There is another job out there waiting for you. If you will use your previous experiences as a learning process, that will lead you to become more mature and wiser in looking for better opportunities.
2. Keep looking. Send your resumes. There is plenty of support and lots of services available if you need help with your resume or job search.
3. Stretch your remaining budget. Ask for help if necessary. Learn to better prepare yourself next time; something like this has to happen again. Remember, during your most difficult times when as if nothing and nobody else can help, God can be there to carry you through.

E. **H. EVALUATION**: The actions you take will determine the out come. Whatever the situation, don't lose hope nor quit. Learn from every circumstance, it will make you stronger. Finally, brighter days may be just moments away.

See, the PROBLEM SOLVING PROCESS is really that simple. It should not be mistaken with the term "Crisis Intervention," unless you are facing a true crisis, which is obviously not. It is as simple as baking a cake; you start with just a box of flour and a recipe. Get the ingredients and mix them together. Then, you cook it and presto! You have a wonderful dessert. It is like a student dealing with an assignment; it begins with a perplexing question or problem, he gathers his tools to look for the answer, experiments, verifies, finally writing down his best answer, then presto! An A+!

Just like a husband and wife, who normally argue and fight during the early years of their marriage while getting to know each other better (the 'real' them) and adjusting to each other's personality. They learn to calm down and listen to each other, have heart to heart talks, and make up (actually, the best part, remember that; a great spice to a marriage). The process applies to any given situation and is a better way of handling conflicts. If practiced by both parties, they can communicate more objectively and come up with better resolutions they can both be happy with.

Learn to FOCUS on the SOLUTION, not the problem. When you practice this process, it is amazing how much you can learn. The most important lesson to learn is to eventually realize that what you are really facing is not a problem but a SITUATION that can be resolved. Take it as a challenge. Experience how good it feels to be able to say at the end, "Mission Accomplished!"

Just keep practicing this process, IT WORKS! The usual advice you will hear is to start small until you become more comfortable, until you are ready for big things. That is true on most cases. But in case you suddenly have this big dream, as you go through the process and you find your belief comfort and ready to accomplish your BIG DREAMS, I say, GO FOR IT!

What are your challenges? What problems and struggles you need to resolve and aim to have solutions? What obstacles you need to deal with or overcome? Make a decision to do what it will take, and apply the Problem-Solving Process (also called Solution-Achievement Process). It will be so liberating and fulfilling once accomplished.

Remember that the only limitations you have are the limitations you put in front of you. Otherwise, the sky is the limit. Meaning, your opportunity is UNLIMITED as the UNIVERSE!

Once you grasp these principles, you will live your life with UNLIMITED JOY or EXCITEMENT. This time you can call YOUR NAME followed by a loud, "GO FOR IT!" Let's MOVE MOUNTAINS!!

"Believe you can, and you can. Belief is one of the most powerful of all problem dissolvers. When you believe that a difficulty can be overcome, you are more than halfway to victory over it already."
— Norman Vincent Peale, American Writer Minister

My Personal Survival Story

Sometimes I have people tell me, "Easy for you to say because you probably have not experienced real difficult times." I found that this kind of thinking is common among people, the thinking that as if they are the only one going through the difficulties in life, and the others are not. Some live with 'the victim mentality'. On the contrary, all you need to do is get out off your 'self' for a moment and you will notice that people around you all go through tough times.

Tough times and life's challenges come in different shape, form, degree or severity, intensity or duration. I found out that these are natural part of our life and I have not found a single soul yet who is exempt, not even the royalties, celebrities, who supposed to have everything that they could ask for in life – looks, fame and fortune. (So, let's be nice to one another, give each other a break, be more giving and forgiving.) What is important is how we deal with or how we handle these tough situations when they come. Will you come out defeated, or survive and WIN? Remember, most of these situations come without warning, seems like no way you can prepare yourself for some totally unexpected challenges. How prepared or equipped you are, in all aspects of your life – spiritually, mentally, emotionally, physically, socially, financially, can surely be of tremendous help to you. Don't even try to avoid these tests, you may not, no matter what you do. Just have a different positive mindset to shield you as they arise. Just like mistakes and failures, these tough times could bring you closer to your destination. After all, experience is still the best teacher, and practice is the best trainer.

When it comes to tough times, we vary with situations. Here I have a few to share with you:

Being Alone, Away From Home

We were very close as a family. That's why it was not easy for me to be separated from my family when I went to the big city for college. But at the same time, there was a feeling of excitement that I would finally have a taste of independence and see what it was like to be on my own, do whatever I wanted, whenever I wanted to. But it must be those good teachings already embedded in me that kept me from doing foolish things. I had a lot of adventures and fun, and finished college as well. My parents said I did well on my own. I felt good.

It did not occur to me that it could be different the next time. I was very excited about going to America, "the land of milk and honey." I came here without knowing anybody and without knowing anything about my destination: Miami, Florida. In May 1979, together with two other nurses I had met on the plane, we arrived at the Miami airport at night. We immediately called the number the agency gave us to call upon arrival. We were instructed to take a taxi to the address given to us. We arrived at a nursing home.

When we got there, the supervisor made several phone calls and we waited and waited and waited. So tired from that long day and a half journey which involved four connecting flights, I realized when I woke up that I fell asleep in my chair for several hours.

No one seemed to know where we should be going. One of the nurses, who also came from the Philippines, realizing we didn't really have a place to go, invited us to her home. I don't know where she is now, but I will always remember and appreciate "Lolita" for welcoming us to her one-bedroom apartment she was occupying with her American husband. We were very happy to lay our tired backs on their living room floor. They were very nice. They fed us for a couple of days while helping us find an apartment for ourselves and be able to start on our own.

The next day after our arrival, we had an orientation and we were given our work assignment, even before we could find a place to stay and settle in. The housekeeping supervisor told us that she had heard the administrator say, "I don't care if they sleep under the bridge." That was hard for us to believe, although we noticed that she really didn't make any effort to help us find a place to stay, or even asked where we were staying. We then found out that we were working as graduate nurses, responsible for many patients, being paid a minimum wage.

I surely was naive to be caught up with all these unexpected situations. The one-bedroom apartment we were renting was over a mile from the nursing home. That was close if you had a car, but walking back and forth that far each day, sometimes blocked by a barking dog or caught in the rain was not easy.

All the stores were far too, especially so when you did not know where to get the things you needed. Our neighbors, predominantly Latin and some Blacks, were mostly understanding, helpful and seemed to relate to what we were going through. The small amount I was being paid, about $240 every two weeks, was not enough to pay my share of the rent and buy basic necessities, much less send any money to my family back home which was the main reason I dared to be separated this far from them.

Being in a new land with only strangers around, unfamiliar languages spoken, and other experiences I do not particularly wish to even remember, I was lonely, very lonely. I remembered many sleepless nights drenching my pillow with tears. I missed my family and my home. I missed my fiancée and my friends. I missed everything else which were all then impossible to reach. It was not easy for a young lady like me (I was 22) to feel so sad, to feel so alone in such a strange world, not sure of what I could do about it, whom to trust or where I could get help. They told me I was going through a "cultural shock" of some sort.

One day, I simply decided, "Enough of being depressed. Get up and see what you can do." I decided to go to a nearby church even by myself. Somehow it eased the pain I was going through. Although the people were strangers at first, they welcomed me well. The Bible study teacher, "Grace," offered her home to me. She is a single mother of two beautiful girls and is a wonderful lady. She helped me to understand a lot of things and to cope better. I will never forget her. She must have been God-sent. Things began to work out better after that.

I transferred to a small hospital nearby three months after my arrival, to the great anger of the nursing home director who threatened to deport me if I didn't come back. I still remember what I told her, "Go ahead, I want to go home anyway. And don't threaten me, I know how the patients are being treated at this nursing home." I never heard from her again. The other hospital petitioned me and paid me more than twice what I was making previously. I was happier with the atmosphere and the patients were treated much better. God had proven to me again that "I am not alone."

"Lonely" is the word I used to describe myself, especially during my first few months. Added to that was the depression of watching the elders in the nursing home on a daily basis, getting limited care, on their wheelchair or bed almost the whole day. Of the three months I was at the nursing home, I probably welcomed less than ten visitors to a hundred residents. I was told that some of them had been there for years without any visits or calls at all. It was very hard for me to imagine what that must be like for them. The word had to be beyond "lonely." It was very difficult for me to take that and as I tried to talk to some of them, they were so unresponsive and lifeless, as if they had not been talked to for ages or maybe were just over sedated. It was a sad, scary feeling that I could not take for long.

In the neighborhood were other immigrants like myself. I found out later that many were refugees who had escaped their countries from nearby islands and were finding refuge in America. Imagine being both *lonely* and *scared* at the same time. Most of them did not have any relatives to welcome them, no jobs waiting, limited or no food to eat and afraid that the immigration service might come at anytime and deport them. Who was I to complain?

I have to admit that what I had seen and experienced during those first months was not the picture I had in my mind about America. Was I somehow mistakenly transported to the wrong place? Was this really America? Don't take me wrong, I realized later that America is really beautiful and one of the best places in the world to be. But at that time, I am sure I was not alone in my disillusionment.

Exactly one year later, my fiancée was able to follow me. I was definitely not alone anymore. We did very well together, and had three beautiful children right in a row. I have mentioned our humble accomplishments in our business, which I would have thought impossible. We had no business background whatsoever. It must be that the "free-enterprise system" in America really works. All I know is that *impossible things can be possible.*

Everyone has his or her own sad or lonely moments. That, apparently, will always come to visit us. The point is, don't lose hope, keep going, and give your best. Keep your dreams alive. Be open to opportunities, and when you are given one, GO FOR IT! It may be just the right one for you. Life is filled with challenges and adventures. Life is wonderful in its rewards. Life is meaningful with its battles to be won.

Wherever you are, whatever your situation, with God, you are never alone.

Losing Someone So Dear

The death of my parents, one after the other, were among the most painful period of my life. Probably for any of us, to lose someone dear is very painful, especially when it comes at the worst moment in your life when you feel so helpless, so useless. (My other book, *Yes, The Secrets Work,* gave more details of my personal life challenges. I'm sharing here some.)

Others Are Also Experiencing Loss

While I can think only of my own losses, as if I was alone, there are apparently so many other people experiencing losses in various ways. That's what life is about. While some are celebrating, some are grieving. While some are gaining or winning, others are experiencing major losses. While some people are laughing, some are crying. While some are dying, new birth continues. Life goes on.

I occasionally still remember my parents, our trials and ordeals. I still cry sometimes, and the more I am able to express it, the less the burden or pain becomes. This must be the HEALING PROCESS. Most of all, I know that I must go on, as "life goes on," especially for the sake of our children. Focusing on our children's welfare helped a lot. Focusing on God, His love and purpose for us, made our life more meaningful and complete. Even when more trials come, I can now say that: "the chapter in our life is not yet finished."

Facing Death

Since both of my parents had died of cancer at an early age, I thought it would not hurt to have a physical check-up even if I was feeling alright. So, I scheduled myself for a complete check up, including a pap test for the first time in my life at age thirty-eight.

Who would think that on my very first pap test, the doctor would discover "multiple abnormal cells." I was immediately scheduled for a series of tests to ascertain what it was. A repeat pap test indicated the same thing. A colposcopy, on which a biopsy was taken, confirmed the test results.

How was I supposed to react to all this? It was my very first test and I did not expect them to find anything abnormal. Was it cancer or not? That was unthinkable. I was too young (at least that's how I felt). My children were still too young. We were in the process of moving into our new home, and as soon as we were settled I was going to get a job to help my husband. That was our plan. My doctor said I had to have a minor surgery to remove those cells and prevent them from progressing. Why now? All kinds of questions and thoughts ran through my mind. I started remembering my previous patients at the oncology unit. I know the disease process and what most of them had to go through.

Somehow I was not afraid and told myself, "Just one of those things I have to deal with, what else." I found out I could face death if that's where I was headed. I know life is short. Mine has been extended several times. That's why I always try to do my best, trying not to waste any time. I felt ready to face my Creator. I couldn't wait. I know heaven is *heaven*. It must be wonderful there, "no more tears, no more pain, no more sorrow." I'd been through enough pain, tears and sorrow and I wouldn't mind a good rest. Part of me was excited (somehow). It must sound crazy to some, but heaven surely is better than life on earth, if you really know that is where you are going.

In the meantime I had to think of my husband and my children, too. I cannot stop death. I know that. And when my time comes, no one can stop it, except God of course, if He wills it. But I wanted to be prepared. My life insurance was current, so at least there is something for them to carry on with. Can you believe that I even wrote a letter to my husband "of things to do, just in case"? I told him that out of the insurance to pay-off all our remaining debts, give a little to my sisters, brothers, to my mother-in-law, and to a few others. The rest is for him and the children and their college education. Also included was "where things are." All I could think of was, "I might as well prepare so my husband won't have such a hard time." I laughed at myself, but I will not deny that tears wet my cheeks too.

That's when I thought about writing this book. You never know what will happen next. I am leaving that to God. It doesn't really matter. Whenever and wherever I will be, I am happy, knowing I will always be with the Lord, and He is always with me. I have peace because I am assured that my family will be all right as well.

What about those who have been actually diagnosed with heart disease, cancer, and other serious illnesses? What about them? Have you not heard of people who were diagnosed, and were supposed to have a great chance of recovery, but because of their fear or depression, died earlier? Be aware that fear and depression can be deadlier than the illness itself. A person may not have any illness and can still suddenly die, or cut his life short because of emotional downfalls or other non-medical factors.

On the other hand, there are those who have been diagnosed with deadly diseases and illnesses, yet continue to live their normal lives, go to work, travel and play - for as they say, "When it comes, it comes. For now I will live my remaining days to the fullest." And they do. Findings show that they live longer than expected. When they die, relatives and friends say, "He LIVED a good life, a happy and fruitful life" as opposed to, "He DIED just like that, in misery." Did you notice how on both occasions of death, two different words were used; and the way those words were used?

Some people even recover completely. They call it a "miracle," something that the medical world cannot fully explain, but now accept and even encourage people to have faith and pray, for it may be their only chance. It should not come as a surprise to know that majority of those in the medical profession actually believe in God and miracles. Did you know that many doctors, nurses and other health workers are more comfortable working when they know they are being prayed for? We surely trust an excellent doctor, why can't we trust an awesome God?

How do you view "death"? Isn't it just a part of our life, just like we talk about "birth"? What is so scary about death, or is it rather what is not known about it that makes one scared? Some can celebrate the occasion of death as "life on earth ended," just like a "welcomed birth." It boils down again to the way we live our life as a whole being, the way we think, feel, etc. We need to learn to really "live" a healthy, happy, victorious life... no matter what.

Let me share with you a very popular chapter in the Book of Life that has meant a lot to me. I first heard it from my Uncle Nino, whom, at a young age working as a presidential guard, was shot about twenty times during an encounter. Four bullets seriously injured him, which he survived, but left him a paraplegic and bound to a wheelchair. He still somehow managed to be married happily to a beautiful and truly incredible wife, Raquel. For me, Uncle Nino is incredible, too. He even had the opportunity to come to America. His life had been amazing. During one of my visits with him at the hospital, while I was still in college, he shared this chapter with me. He said he memorized it because it helped him a lot while he was on the verge of dying. I want to share it with you because, who knows, someday it may mean something to you, too.

Psalm 23 (NKJV)

The Lord is my Shepherd I shall not
    want
He makes me to lie down in green
    pastures
He leads me beside the still waters
He restores my soul

He leads me in the paths of
    righteousness
For His name's sake.

<u>Yea, though I walk through the valley of</u>
    <u>the shadow of death</u>
<u>I will fear no evil</u>
<u>For You are with me</u>
<u>Your rod and Your staff, they</u>
    <u>comfort me.</u>
You prepare a table before me in the
    presence of my enemies
You anoint my head with oil
My cup runs over.
Surely goodness and mercy shall
    follow me
All the days of my life
And I will dwell in the house of the Lord
Forever.

Life is like a weather forecast. Most of the time we know what may be coming and we can plan for it. Sometimes, we just can't tell and our plans fall apart.

Life has its seasons, too. Sometimes it is gloomy and unpredictable (autumn); sometimes it is cold and treacherous (winter); followed by refreshing new days (spring), and next of course, the bright and sunny days (summer). This is a cycle that never fails to occur as long as we live. Knowing that the four seasons have a remarkable similarity with the events in our lives, awareness of its nature helps us to be more prepared and increases our ability to survive. Most importantly, remember: When the going gets tough, apply your new gained knowledge and natural abilities to survive and rest assured that sunny days will soon to follow.

Life is made up of magnificent wonders and miracles. Let me share with you another such event in my life.

A Sudden Storm

It was a beautiful day indeed in a magnificent small island in the Philippines. The medical team decided to take four of us volunteers on a stroll around the island after a long day of clinic work. There were two medical students and two nursing students who volunteered for two weeks on that remote island of about thirty families. I was assigned to provide health education to the residents. It was our last day there. Our host was busy preparing a very special dinner for us. We had become very close to them, even in such a short period of time.

I will never forget that day. About five in the afternoon after work, we strolled the shallow coral reef surrounding the island. It was so beautiful! With water up to my knees, I could see different live corals of all kinds of magnificent shapes and colors, which were a delight to inspect with curious eyes. There were small colorful fishes I had never seen before, which were also fascinating. I felt I could stay there forever.

I was enjoying my exploration by myself when I heard people calling my name, "Leah!" The team was beginning to ride on a couple of wooden canoes to go around the island. I ran to them and practically jumped into the seat they saved for me. This would be my first experience to ride a canoe and I was very excited. The past two weeks had truly been an adventure of a lifetime for me.

There were three people in each canoe. In ours was the volunteer male resident doctor who would do the paddling, another student nurse, and myself. It was about 5:30 in the afternoon, and it was still sunny with bright blue sky. The water was very calm and crystal clear. We could see many magnificent things under the clear blue water. As we paddled along, it was fascinating to look at the small waves splash against the isolated big rocks near the beach. It was such a wonderful experience and time flies in moments like this one.

After almost an hour, we were heading back to the shore. I saw the first team had already reached the beach. We were following close

77

behind them. But then I noticed that instead of getting closer to the shore, we were going farther and farther away. I also noticed that the waves were getting bigger and higher as dark clouds suddenly rushed into our area. In minutes it became dark, and heavy raindrops began to pour down. We were very quiet, wondering what was happening. The waves were getting bigger and bolder, and I saw that we were getting closer and closer to the big rocks. As we were headed towards the rocks, I thought it would surely smash our canoe and ourselves as well. The paddles were useless. We did not know what to do.

Then I felt a big wave lift us towards the sky and toss our canoe back into the ocean. I felt myself sinking under the water with my eyes closed. When I opened my eyes underwater, all I saw was my slipper in front of me and the other one still on my other foot. I immediately grabbed the slipper, as there was nothing else there to cling onto. As a nursing student, I was required to know how to swim. I tried to remain calm and just float. With my head above water gasping for air, I looked around. I could not see much at all since it was raining so hard. The waves were very treacherous and it was totally dark. I could not see anything or anybody. I did not know what to think at first.

I began talking to myself, "How could this happen?" Where were my companions?" Then I heard a male voice (which I recognized) calling, "Leah! Josephine!" That was Rey, the volunteer resident doctor. Although I could not see him, I knew he was not that far from me. I cried, "I'm here!" and started swimming towards where I thought the voice was coming from. I found Rey clinging to the overturned canoe. Then I saw Josephine swimming towards it with obvious difficulty. Rey went to help her. We were all glad to see each other still alive.

We just hung on to the canoe. We tried to turn it over, but couldn't. We stayed there hanging on for a very long time, as the storm continued to do its task.

Hours must have passed. We did not say anything to each other, probably because the noise of the storm was so loud and conversation was impossible. Or possibly it was because we really did not know what to say to each other at that moment, or we were simply busy thinking, "What will happen to us?" "How are we going to survive this?" We had no means of calling for help, and who would hear us anyway? It also occurred to me that the small island had no rescue team, no telephone, not even electricity for light. Survival seemed impossible at the time. All we could do was pray.

So, did we survive the storm? Of course we did and I am very glad to be alive to tell you about it. As I share my personal life stories with you, I sincerely hope they can help you in some way.

What Helped Us Survive The Storm?

How did my two companions and I survive the unexpected storm? Especially when we knew that help could not be expected, and that we did not have any means or idea of how to help ourselves get out of the situation. It was a point in time where we had to face our own limitations. At this point, it did not matter if Rey's parents were rich and could pull all sources of help if they only knew what was happening. It would not even matter if Josephine and I got A's in our P.E. for swimming and that we were trained to be resourceful. We remained calm (somehow), but all we could do was WAIT for whatever would come next.

We floated that way for hours, holding on to the canoe, while rain continued to pour down and waves kept bouncing us around. I remember wondering why it seemed like there was a light at our immediate site. I say that because I could not see anything at all beyond my perimeter. It was total darkness, and I had no idea where we were in that large ocean. I could not see any sign of the island or anything else nearby. Yet I could see my companion's faces clearly, the canoe, and my feet under the water in their waving motion. Where was that light coming from? That thought diverted my attention for some time. Then we noticed a canoe with a man in it, alone, someone I did not recognize, coming towards us. He could not come any closer because of the waves. I heard Rey yell out that we could not turn the canoe over. The next thing I saw was the man throwing a rope to Rey and yelling to him to tie it onto our canoe, which Rey did as he found a spot to tie it. After the rope was secured, he sat down and started paddling, pulling us (and the canoe) wherever he was headed. I presumed he was one of the men on the island and he was taking us there. It took a long time. He must have been a very strong person and well skilled to have been able to find us, tackle the storm and pull us to safety. I could not help wondering, "How was he able to find us in such big, dark and stormy ocean?"

The storm subsided as we approached the island. Everyone on the island was at the shore when we got there. They hugged us and gave us blankets. Some of our co-workers were crying. They had been so worried and praying for us, they said. We dried ourselves, ate some supper and finally went to bed. I looked at my watch and saw that the time was after midnight. My prayer for thanksgiving to God was brief but very meaningful and I slept well till dawn.

We were scheduled to leave the island very early that morning. The motorboat from the main island arrived on time, even before we could get ready. It was amazing to see the blue sky and calm blue ocean again that morning, as if nothing at all had happened the night before. The three of us were all perfectly fine.

I thought everyone on the island was there that morning to say good-bye to us. In all the rush and commotion, I realized later that we left without having a chance to meet face to face with the person who came to our rescue, and thank him. I did not even know his name.

I brought some souvenirs with me, mainly coral and shells, which I treasured but found out later that I could not always keep or carry them with me. But the precious memories of our two weeks on that island will always be with me wherever I go. I will never be able to forget those very simple but very warm-hearted, hospitable natives of the island. I will, of course, never forget our last night there, which could have been our very last but apparently not. There is no year that passes by that I do not recall that night. Each year, the memory gives me new insight, new meaning, a new lesson in life. It was apparently meant to be a very significant prelude to my coming adventures in life.

What had helped us during the storm, and what may also help you during your challenging times in life? There are three important things to learn from this story:

- **KNOWLEDGE** - Applying what I had learned from our swimming lessons, especially staying calm and afloat, surely helped a great deal while we were in the middle of the ocean. It is the knowledge gathered over the years from study and experience that carries us through the real tough times.

Knowledge is a very valuable part of our lives. That is why we go to school and spend many hours a day, and years of our lives, to get an "education." EDUCATION, as the dictionary defines, *is a systematic training and instruction designed to impart knowledge and develop skill*, which is what our schools are for. KNOWLEDGE, on the other hand, *is the body of information; all that a person knows*, which we gather not only from our schools, but especially from our everyday life experiences where all the information can be verified, tested and applied. Besides the schools, we gain knowledge from our homes, churches, institutions, various associations we have, seminars, people we meet or observe, and situations we encounter every day. Knowledge becomes even more meaningful when it is appreciated, tested, applied and shared. Knowledge is like *a backpack of supplies* that you carry with you wherever you go and is available to use whenever you need to. It will always be there to help you and to guide you.

KNOWLEDGE is a valuable treasure to seek out and keep, a treasure that no one can take away from you. The amount of knowledge you gather determines how equipped you are and how prepared you are to face life, to survive and enjoy it. The question really is, *"Is your backpack of knowledge half-full or half-empty?"* The knowledge you have now will help you answer that.

I was just thinking of MY PARENTS, all the love that they gave me and the "good lessons" they taught me. I loved them so much, but how many times did I express that, on how much I appreciated everything they did for me. I have since learned to be more expressive, of more important things to express. Wherever you are Dad, Mom, "I love you!" and "Thank you!" "You are the best parents I can have."

I wish to thank all my TEACHERS and ALMA MATER as well. I can easily recall my good teachers from elementary school to college. They were "good" because they were dedicated and you could tell that they really cared. They surely made a contribution in molding my life and my future. I want to give a special commendation to my college alma mater, Philippine Christian University-Mary Johnston College of Nursing. Any graduate from that college will be proud to tell you that since its founding, 100% of her graduates have passed the National Nurses Board Exams. As I look back, I realize that is not the only reason why we are proud of our school and kept a special bond with all the graduates. Our teachers were definitely good, but most of all, they genuinely cared about us, not just for our "future success in a career," but for each individual's general welfare and wellbeing. The way they taught us and cared for is something we can then carry on throughout our lifetime. More than just the technical aspects of nursing, they taught us and exposed us to experience the real meaning of brotherhood (and sisterhood), the fellowship of men and women, of LOVE and COMPASSION, which are the very essence of humanity. The school is like a home of a very big family. We all share and carry this feeling even now during our reunions at school and wherever else we may go. Some of my friends don't comprehend this when I tell them that our local school graduates meet once or twice a year, with reunion attendees from the graduates of 1940s to the present, and we always have a great time, just like being at a family reunion.

To my alma mater and to all my teachers, *"Thank you!" "You made a very positive difference in my life."*

A Big THANKS to the many speakers at the different seminars, conferences and conventions I have attended. I truly learned a lot. To many other people whom I have watched and listened to, and who were unaware and will never realize the precious moments they have shared with me, and to everyone, "THANK YOU!" The KNOWLEDGE I gathered through all of you is immeasurable.

- **PEOPLE WHO CARE** - If you noticed, *knowledge* is not just a bunch of information we can refer to as the "technical know-how." Of equal importance is the WHO's, as true knowledge acknowledges that we are *human beings*, not robots or machines. What makes our life beautiful is the knowledge that there are PEOPLE WHO CARE; people who are willing to share and to sacrifice, for the sake of others. Firefighters are a great example of people who are ready to risk their own lives for other's sake. Whoever the man was who came to our rescue in the ocean surely risked his life to save us. He must be an extension of God's hand. Some people call such a person "an angel" sent from above. It must be, for God is the very first and the greatest example of such a graceful act of love and sacrifice. I cannot help being reminded of God's love to us that He gave His only son to sacrifice on the cross and die for us so we can live. God continues to further extend His mercy through other people. I sincerely thank that man who came to our rescue, for being God's instrument of mercy and power.

With so many storms that we had been through, there were people who, knowingly or unknowingly, were there for us to extend kindness, comfort, understanding, and much more. There was my sister and best friend, Bella, and some other relatives. They were the neighbors, schoolmates, workmates, and various groups and organizations I have belonged to. I also wish to thank the ministers and pastors, the church leaders and the wonderful members of the different churches that we have visited, and their guest speakers who unselfishly shared their lives so that others could benefit. They all have become our extended families and extensions of God's tender mercies.

Each one of us needs these caring people, and they are all there, ready to help. And just as important, that there are people out there who need to know YOU CARE.

- **BELIEVING in GOD'S UNFAILING LOVE** - There are those moments that even with all the gathered knowledge, caring people, and all the resources available to us, nothing helps us more during our most desperate moments, or periods of limitations, than the knowledge and assurance that God knows, that He is always there for us. God is more than just a friend who really cares and loves us.

I found out more about God and His love for us through His Son, Jesus, when I was sixteen. Although I occasionally attended church, I never really knew Him on a personal basis. He revealed Himself to me, that He *is* real, when I was a freshman in college. I made my decision then to surrender my life to Him, to be my Lord and Savior forever. Our personal Father-child relationship has been more than meaningful. It has been wonderful! I will not deny that there were times when I have set Him aside for some distractions in life but, as I stumble, I kept coming back to Him and He always lovingly welcomes me back (just like the story of the "Prodigal Son").

The tough times I have been through helped me learn to completely FOCUS on Him, His ways, His will, and put my full trust in Him alone. How else did we survive and have continued to survive well no matter what? We LIVED BY FAITH IN GOD, in His Word, in His Promises. *"And the Lord, He is the One who goes before you. He will be with you, He will not leave you nor forsake you; do not fear nor be dismayed."* (Deuteronomy 31:8) *"Yet in all these things we are MORE THAN CONQUERORS through Him who loved us."* (Romans 8:37) To anyone who contradicts those words or tries to persuade me otherwise, I simply reply, "What better alternative do you have?"

BELIEVING goes beyond knowledge. It creates wonders and miracles beyond a man's ability to comprehend.

BELIEVING does not cost us anything, but it has been proven to be MORE PRECIOUS than any treasure and MORE POWERFUL than any armor available here on earth.

QUESTIONS:

"With your backpack of knowledge, did you include the knowledge that *God truly loves you,* that He cares for anything and everything about you?"

"Is your backpack for survival in life filled with *belief* that you surely CAN make it?"

BELIEVE, because with God, NOTHING IS IMPOSSIBLE!

Chapter 4

Life Can Be Better Understood and Lived

Could it be that people are lost or suffer because of lack of knowledge?

*L*ife is wonderful! Life is colorful, truly beautiful... if you can relate to what I am talking about. A lot of people don't see it that way. They are still so wrapped up with the life complexities and challenges, and without much understanding of the nature of what they are dealing with or how to go about these challenges, life surely can bogged one down.

Realize that 'life is not a bed of roses,' as the usual saying goes. Come to think of it, as beautiful as the roses are, people sometimes forget that this favorite flower comes with thorns, that can hurt if you are not careful or have not learned how to deal with them. Life can be better understood. **Life**...

- is **A PROCESS**. We can better appreciate our life in comparison to precious gems or metals, like a diamond or gold, which need to go through the refining process to get to its best form for best value and appreciation.
- is **like A WHEEL**. Sometimes you are *up*, sometimes you are *down*. It is a way of life that makes it more beautiful or colorful, once you understand the principle. How can you go anywhere if the wheel on your vehicle is not moving, up and down? Can you imagine your life with same food, task, etc. Life will be monotonous, people get bored. That's why 'change' is a must and a welcome word to those who understand. The stock market, the making and losing of money, does not exist without the wheel principle. Imagine a person at the intensive care unit with the heart monitor showing a straight line, instead of the up and down flow? This principle is important to keep us and our economy alive and well. So, don't get to scared when things are down (temporarily), because, the GOOD NEWS is, when you reach the bottom, the only other way is, UP!
- **has its SEASON**. Yes, everything around us helps us understand life. You can compare our life to the seasons that we have to go through, whether you like it or not: AUTUMN, is when our days begin to be gloomy; then comes the challenging cold WINTER; then the beautiful SPRING comes like a fresh new beginning, full of colors and fresh new leaves on once seemingly dead or bare trees; then comes SUMMER full of sunshine, when people comes out to enjoy the sun! Regardless of the season, if you understand and see what are the best things you can get or do out of every situation, every season or situation has something good to offer. This is the reason why people go out and enjoy the snow during WINTER instead of just hibernating at home. Same with a

true real estate investor who is having a ball purchasing his investment properties while the rest are feeling gloomy about the RE market. It is *how* you *make the best out of every situation* that you can come out WINNING in life.

To follow are some of much detailed explanation which can help bring some light to our search for LIFE.

The Way of Life

This section hopes to give you some understanding on *why were we who we were, and why are we what we are now?* It will also give some insights as to what you and I can still be. Interestingly, the more you understand your SELF, the more you will understand the OTHERS also and what goes around us in relation to each other on a daily basis.

Have you ever seen a newborn baby that looks devilish? I don't think so. At least, I haven't. They all look so cute, sweet little angels, so adorable, so harmless and cuddly. But what happens after some years? How come some grow up to be so different?

You see, as a child is born and begins to grow and develop, he is like a "dry sponge" that hungrily and willingly absorbs everything that is given or presented to him. Besides his natural genes from his parents, everything that he takes in affects his growth and development. The food that he eats, his environment – including everything that he sees, hears, feels, and the significant people who provide for him, will register in his mental and emotional processes. The adequacy or lack of stimulation and of meeting his basic needs physically, mentally, emotionally, spiritually, and socially, will greatly determine how well the child will adapt in life.

Children are called mimics or "copycats" because that's how they learn, THEY COPY! They exhibit and express what they were 'programmed' to do. The first 3 years, considered the most critical stage of one's life, is all absorption. So do not think that babies and toddlers are unaware, they are. That is why it is very important to be careful of what we expose them to. This is also the reason why toddlers question a lot. (Development ages, by the way, vary for each individual – some develop earlier, some later). Lots of LOVE to develop the sense or feeling of SECURITY at this early stage is very important. At 4-7 years, children are still very responsive to cueing, directions, instructions, and guidance. This is the best time to teach vital information, to reinforce values. So let us not be too hard on our children; they are but a mirror or reflection of their environment.

89

What you may also find interesting is that each child from birth exhibits natural or innate abilities – to adapt, to learn and to develop. Isn't it fascinating to watch an infant opens his mouth and turn his head towards his mother's nipple when he is hungry, even with his eyes closed? Then watch that incredible sucking reflex begin to work. It's incredible! Mind you, no one has to teach him that. Thank God, because even a genius or a Pediatric expert would have a hard time teaching a baby such an important survival step. Another is the natural instinct to blink when a foreign object approaches or gets in the eye, causing tears to naturally flow to try to wash it out. There is the coughing reflex, or the body cells ability to reproduce, etc. These are just few of *the wonders of our being.* Of course, we have the scientific and medical explanations, but still, where do all these marvelous abilities come from? We have these *natural abilities* since childhood, naturally *built in.* It could not just disappear, right? Did we forget, or we allowed somebody to steal or distract us?

By the time the child is 8-13 years old, he tends to become more selective of what to willingly take or what to reject as he begins to develop independence. This is good and should be encouraged with proper care and guidance.

During teenage years, when the child is 13-19, he no longer accepts being called a child. He would rather be recognized as a *young adult* or more appropriate a *teen*. At this time, it is natural for him to feel that he already knows everything. (The best way to understand our children at this stage is simply to recall how we were at that time). After all, his sponge is pretty much filled up with things he has seen, heard and felt. He figures he has everything he needs to be able to be on *his own.* This is the time the teen needs to learn that along with the independence he is beginning to claim, there comes a great deal of *responsibility.* When he was a young child, he was very much dependent on his parents and other adults around him. The parents and those adults *were responsible* for him. But as the child grows and declares independence, he has to learn and begin to accept responsibility and *accountability* for his own decisions and actions. With the independence, the teen still needs continuous guidance in making the choices and decisions. When he becomes an adult, or as soon as he assumes full independence, he will carry along those lessons with him. If we adults fail to teach our children RESPONSIBILITY and ACCOUNTABILITY, it is chaos. Pointing fingers, blaming others does not work.

From the early teens to about 25, life is an interesting adventure, a true learning process. After experimenting with and testing what the individual knows, or thinks he knows, the young learner now begins to sort, to validate and to evaluate if the information he got is actually good or bad for him. Those who have received good nurturing or good programming early in life can adjust to society better and faster, with feelings of security and confidence. Those who did not, will have more difficulty adjusting because there is still so much to sort out. Confusion, anger, rebellion or regression may be demonstrated. A feeling of insecurity, and lack of confidence or trust in oneself or others may be experienced, making it a very difficult time for those who are in this situation. Violent crimes, movies, TV shows, video games, magazines and other forms of media, expose our children to more unwanted predicaments. Come to think of it, it is becoming a concern for what type of world we are molding now. High divorce rate, conflicts and violence even among family members are reflection of the effect of previous 'programming'.

Two situations may arise in this particular case. First, the dangerous side is for those who simply say, "I give up. This is what I am and this is what I will be." The second, on more positive side, may say, "This may be my situation now, but I can make it different. I am not a hopeless case." We have already heard a lot of people who were branded as 'born on the wrong side of town' or 'who have no hope or future'. But these great men and women stood up, fought, persevered and made a huge difference in their lives, and eventually shared the same opportunity and success as others.

Things can change. PEOPLE CAN CHANGE. In fact, as much as we resist it, CHANGE is one for sure that is constant. CHANGE for the BETTER is always good! It is a matter of DECISION, what a person chooses to take, to do, to follow. This is what you call REPROGRAMMING or RECONDITIONING. A person at any age between 20 to 40 or even younger, as soon as he becomes fully aware of what or who he is, can assume responsibility for his life's direction. He can now decide what to take and keep, or what to reject or delete from his program. He can reshape and reprogram his future to what it will be or what he can be. It can be done, if the person chooses to, especially if a supportive environment is available.

"Life begins at 40," is a saying that seems to fit the assumption that, by that age, experiences should have thought us enough lessons to gain wisdom. We now have a better chance to live our lives the way it should be. Do our children really have to wait that long and go through the things we have been through before they learn important life's basic principles?

LEARNING is an endless process. Even college graduates have not yet finished their schooling, at least not in the real arena of life. Learning goes on as life goes on. Even our seniors can still learn. It is never too late for anyone. Each can still grow and develop more mature, learn new skills, learn better ways to make life worth living. Yes, just be an OPEN door for more and greater opportunities. After all, this is the way of life.

In fact, learn to RELAX, learn to SING and DANCE, learn your best SMILE, LAUGH, learn to LIVE with PASSION ... LIVE to your FULLEST POTENTIAL!

> *"Always be a first-rate version of yourself, instead of a second-rate version of somebody else."*
> – Judy Garland, singer

Life as a Puzzle

Life is like a PUZZLE. When you open the box and see the hundred or thousand pieces all jumbled together, it seems so hopelessly complicated, it is almost impossible to imagine putting it together. In fact, some will hesitate or refuse to even try right there. Just like this book, each section or chapter remains as a piece of the puzzle until you read its entirety. You can then visualize the total picture, that everything in it actually fits together. Sometimes, life is so complex and puzzling, but in the end, it all makes sense.

Putting one's life together can be likened to putting a puzzle together. If you work at it, allow enough time and perseverance, it can be done. Once you are familiar with the pieces, it becomes a lot easier. To put the pieces of your puzzle of life together, you need to take the following steps:

1. GAIN SOME KNOWLEDGE. Learn the basics of life. Learn how to sort out the pieces and how to put them together, Apply what you have learned.

2. LEARN TO ORGANIZE and PRIORITIZE. Let's take a typical puzzle picture of a barn in a field in mid-spring, all jumbled up in the box. You cannot just randomly pick out pieces and try to put them together. It is harder and takes much longer to do it that way. First, put the colors together. The flowers and

greens together, the reds or browns for the barn, the blues and whites for the sky, etc. Remember, each piece and each group is important and actually represents something. These groups of colors represent the positives and the good things in life. Always focus on them first, then you will find it easier to put your puzzle of life together. The black or dark pieces that seem to show nothing, what about them? Of course, that is what it seems, but they are needed, too. Those are the dark periods of our life, trials included, which are somehow necessary to make the picture, our life, complete. They will eventually accent the colors in our life. For how can we appreciate the brighter sides of life – love, joy and peace, if we do not experience some dark sides – test, trials, sadness, loneliness? It would be a dull, meaningless life.

3. LEARN TO PERSEVERE. Life's challenges are so many and so often it would be easy to quit before the fruits of our labor are realized. But if one perseveres and overcomes adversity, a wonderful outcome can be achieved.

When the puzzle picture is complete, like when a goal is achieved, you will find that it is not really impossible to put together a 'masterpiece', YOU, your life. It is amazing to find that those separate pieces that looked so confusing now make sense and actually fit together. That, apparently, everything we go through in life, everything about us and around us, ALL FITS.

Practical Application:

As you work on your personal puzzle of life, picture that barn in the field on a beautiful day in spring. Now as you organize the pieces together according to their color classification, you will also remember what each group represents in your life. FOCUS on these three:

1. The BARN – your STORAGE of BLESSINGS. What are they?

2. The FIELD – your GIFTS, SPECIAL TALENTS and SKILLS. What are they?

3. The BLUE SKY and WHITE CLOUDS – your GOALS, DREAMS, WISHES. What are they?

The BARN, or your storage of blessings is your storage of strength and source of security. Each of us has something to put on the list, so count all your blessings inside that barn, everything that you have that you are thankful for. Remind yourself of how blessed you really are. Even if you think you have nothing to be thankful for, the fact that you are alive is actually a blessing. That means God is not finished with you yet. Keep your hope, your faith that something good is about to happen, that something good is in store for you. Open the door and windows of your barn, look up to the sky, and ask for His blessings to pour upon you – not just money, but health, happiness, peace, wisdom, etc. If you truly believe, are willing to wait, and you continue to strive as He leads you, then you can expect God to deliver for you.

The FIELD or garden with scattered FLOWERS represents your God-given talents and special gifts that were uniquely designed and given to you. They also include the skills you have acquired. Like the plants and flowers, they need to be discovered, identified, and nurtured for one to fully enjoy their beauty and benefits. Don't be shy, bring them out. Find out what you are good at, what you are interested in and develop these talents and skills. You will find that these assets can help bring meaning to your life. Eventually, you will be able to share your gifts with others and fulfill your life's purpose.

The BLUE SKY and WHITE CLOUDS represent your goals, dreams and wishes which, like the sky, is endless. Have you heard of the phrase "The sky is the limit"? That means your realm of opportunity is actually endless and has no boundaries. Mistakes, failures or even the most difficult trials should neither stop you nor slow you down. Arise and embrace the challenges of life. While you are still alive, there are still a lot more doors for you to open, more options and opportunities for you to discover. Go on, pursue your dreams, your goals, your wishes. They are there for a purpose. Consider this phrase, *"Whatever your mind can conceive and believe, you can achieve" by Napoleon Hill.* It is as simple as thinking about eating a delicious ice cream, and then going to the freezer or store to make that happen. It is as possible as the man who dreamed of stepping on the moon. His impossible dream became a reality. Yes, the only thing that is stopping you from achieving your goals, dreams and wishes is the limitations that you place in front of you. Think about it.

Do not worry about those dark pieces or vague spots of the puzzle – the test and trials. They are part of the puzzle of life. You can overcome these. Most of the time they are difficult, but they will not last. Sooner or later, they will find their perfect fit or spot of importance. Sometimes we ourselves feel like we are on the dark spot or in the dark, but after awhile we realize that, that point of time is very significant to our journey of life. At times, tough times and impossible situations may simply be an indication that you need to be flexible and be open to other possibilities. It could mean using another piece of the puzzle or trying out another spot, it may be time to change your thinking or use a new approach. It may take time, but somewhere, somehow, the piece of puzzle you are holding will finally fit into the whole picture.

When you get to the point of your limitations, the best thing to do is to seek God's guidance (which is best done actually from the beginning, not just when you are already desperate for help. Thank God, with Him it is never too late and whenever you need Him he is just a call away). Also, do not hesitate to ask others for help. It is not always easy to ask for help, especially for someone who has been 'independent', but it is a wiser step than feeling sorry for yourself or giving up. Relax and stay calm. When you recover and regain your composure, you can refocus your attention on the three positive aspects of life mentioned earlier – your barn, your field of flowers, and your blue sky and white clouds. After a while, when you look once again at your life's puzzle, you will say, "Piece of cake."

PUZZLES, for ages and generations, have continued to challenge and fascinate us, just like LIFE does. Just remember, a puzzle, like life, is meant to be put together patiently. At the end, it brings out a fulfilling, beautiful masterpiece in YOU!

"Believe that life is worth living, and your belief will help create the fact."
       – William James, American Psychologist & Philosopher

The Truth Can Set You Free (at last!)

There is nothing better in life than to be FREE! FREEDOM remains a universal human drive. Unfortunately, a lot of people remain blind or confused about what 'freedom' really means. Do you have real freedom? Freedom implies the absence of hindrance, restraint, confinement, or repression. To be FREE is wonderful, if it is true freedom. The truth is, FREEDOM is not only *physical*, but also *mental, emotional, spiritual, social* and *financial*. Otherwise, it can be just a clever disguise of what actually is path to destruction. People do a lot of incredible, sometimes even crazy things to attain what they call "freedom". What good is it if you are dead, in prison, a fugitive or living a life of emptiness or misery? Is that freedom? Something is wrong. Someone is lying to you, to us.

The TRUTH can set you FREE! Take note that there is a pre-requisite to true freedom, the TRUTH. Even in court, when the truth prevails, the fate of the suspect's freedom or imprisonment can be determined. Imprisoned or not, the true guilty one will still continuously to be hunted by the truth. If you really want to live a life with freedom and peace, to live a truly meaningful and victorious life, then seek and embrace the TRUTH. It is unfortunate that we are now living in a big world of lies. These lies are designed to distract your attention and divert your focus from the real truth, from what is really good for you. The master deceiver of this world whose job is to constantly influence people has only one purpose: To lead people to self-destruction.

The *evil master* or the *thief* of this world is cunning and manipulative. It is so good at giving negative or destructive suggestions that they are almost unnoticeable. It uses people and circumstances. It knows your weaknesses. It knows exactly how, where and when to attack in such a subtle way that most of the time, you will not know that your situation is his doing until it is too late. Remember that this evil manipulator does not care about you at all, but it is so good at pretending he does. In the end, it laughs at people's foolishness, for the destruction he has caused. It always has, it always will. The Book of Life says *"We do not wrestle against flesh and blood, but against principalities, against powers, against the rulers of the darkness of this age..."* If you do not know what I am talking about, open your eyes and find out more about it, for it is real. It is reality. (You will find The Book of Life reference at the end portion of this book).

Either that same liar masters your life and wins in bringing you to destruction, or stand firm and reclaim your life and the beautiful things that it is trying to steal from you. Win the battle and live the abundant life that you ought to have. The Book of Life says, *"The thief does not come except to steal and to kill and to destroy..."* Suicide, homicide and divorce are just three of the undesirable results that rob us of our dreams and joy, destroy relationships, and destruction when someone gets killed. But the Lord says, *"I have come that you may have life and that you may have it more abundantly."* If we were meant to have an ABUNDANT (joyful, fulfilled, victorious) Life, what is blocking our way from experiencing it? Why there are people who are unhappy, pressured on all sides, trapped, in bondage? Consider this for a moment. Do you have the TRUTH that can SET YOU FREE?

Morals and Family Values are Vital to Life Success

Is this subject even still relevant? For humankind sake, if we still really value our quality of life, then it is relevant. Whatever is happening in our world today, probably even in our own neighborhood is alarming. There is a loud cry for help, for solutions. Should we say, "Let's go re-discover these morals and family values, for they may be the only hope for our society and for our children?" If we say, "Yes," then let's move ahead.

This led me to open my dictionary to find out what is the definition of morals and values. On MORALS, my dictionary says, *of or concerned with the goodness and badness of human character or with the principles of what is right and wrong in conduct; capable of understanding and living by the rules of morality.* On VALUES, it says, *standards or principles considered valuable or important in life.* The presented meanings are simple and self-explanatory, indicative of their relevance in our life.

Next, I went to the library and a bookstore. **Mission: Search for missing morals and values.** I could not help but wonder how many other people out there are doing the same. I found it interesting that there were stacks and stacks of books about computers, success, self-improvement, physical fitness and how to look good, money matters, cookbooks, all kinds of subjects, including those that I believe should not even be in our library in the first place, but close to nothing about morals and family values. No wonder we are missing out. If it is so important, vital to our life, how come there is such a scarcity of resources to gain further knowledge about these subjects? I am curious, for so many years that our children spend in schools from their early childhood, are these subjects even included or incorporated in what they are learning? It is very critical that we answer these questions if we care enough for the present and future generations. Comparing it to the importance of bottled water to most people nowadays, it is like there was an embargo on bottled water and now rarely available. Naturally, people were dying of thirst, so they resorted to drinking even polluted water. Get the picture?

Whose fault is it? Those who think they are smart enough and have no need for morals and family values? Is it the average and ordinary folks who once again gave in to the great old liar of this world? Is it the merchants who introduced all these latest, modern gadgets that seems like we cannot live without, that make us forget what are really more important in our lives? WAKE UP! We all need self-checkups. Obviously, WE ALL must take individual responsibility. We are probably realizing now that no amount of riches, great technology, not even education, modern science and psychology can give us morals and values. It begins from the heart and soul of each individual. What do we choose to think and feel inside? What do you believe?

So where do we and our children learn morals and family values? Shouldn't we learn them from HOME, SCHOOL, CHURCH, and EVERYWHERE else possible? You know the answer to that. SUCCESS and VICTORY in LIFE can be better accomplished by those standing in solid grounds.

What about PRAYER?

When people pray, they believe. And because they believe, MIRACLES happen. When a number of scientists made a study on how miracles happen, they discovered that there are energy forces in this universe that bring together what we believe into reality. In short, something good happens when we pray and believe. So, why stop the flow of good blessings?

Someone who cares gave me the advice that if I want to sell the book, it will be best not to mention things about God, or even prayer. I appreciate such concern, but if I were to follow her advice, there would be no book at all. This is not about religious belief; I am but a 'well-being' advocate. Our government, some schools, and even some homes have stayed away from what they refer as an "issue you do not want to touch." Only now that it is being realized that it has become a national tragedy to stay away from prayers and encouraging the search for a meaningful relationship with God, who is the very source of our existence. It does not matter what people call their Supreme God or how they practice their belief, it remains that we all have basic 'spiritual needs' that need to be met. Has it occurred to us that we call our fathers in different ways, such as "Papa," "Dad," "Pops", Tata," "Tatay," and probably a hundred more other names around the world? Why shy away from the one who magnificently created us all? I have not found anyone yet who truly believes that he or she came from a 'big bang', a microorganism, from animal origin, or whatever else. Do you? Those are theories far from truth, a smart distraction. No matter what, that bang, microorganism, or animal still came from somewhere or someone who created them, right? Because only God is the true beginning and the true end. More and more scientists now are willing to admit that on their futile efforts to discredit God, they but FOUND GOD.

One day I asked my youngest daughter her opinion about 'prayers at school and other public places.' The reply was, "Mom, you know I want prayers at the school, everywhere, but they don't do it because of others' religious beliefs. That seems to be a harmless reason to show 'respect for others.' Doesn't it? I cannot help but remember that at the hospital, there were few incidents when someone refused to receive a blood transfusion because of 'religious belief.' But the hospital did not ban 'blood transfusion' because of that, did they? This LIFE-SAVING NECESSITY is continuously made available to EVERYONE, unless they refuse to receive it, which is their right. The proportion of those who have received and been saved by blood transfusion is far greater than those who refused it. They could have been ALL dead if the hospital had decided to ban blood transfusion out of respect for others beliefs. Yes, 'religious beliefs' is definitely EACH INDIVIDUAL's RIGHT, but is totally different from 'having an opportunity to commune and build a relationship with God', which we all NEED.

Who does not need PRAYER to commune with God? Can your physical body last without food? What will happen to your mind if it is never stimulated or fed with good thoughts? What happens to an individual who never feels love or acceptance, or is banned from feeling or expressing emotions? Can you survive long without working and no money in your pocket? What would it be like for a person to be isolated on an island all by himself? If your spirit is the driving force in your life, shouldn't its need be met as well? Think about it.

Sure, parents and children even at home have different food preferences and eating habits. But in spite of all these differences, it is not a problem. Since food and water are basic necessities, preference is not an issue. Children can amazingly discuss these different practices and preferences with much interest without getting into a fight about them. Let us look at our school settings, especially our public schools. Educators are not the issue here. They are wonderful and greatly appreciated for working so hard to teach our children. The true issue is that someone or something has managed to infiltrate our school system to accomplish its own goal, to remove the means for our children to openly practice meaningful relationship with God and to develop their spirit with good morals and values.

As a result, it should not surprise anyone at all that unthinkable things are now happening in our schools. We can evaluate: *Did the changes made in our schools, in reference to 'removing God and prayers,' caused any good or bad?* Common ground rules of respect can be laid out for the different religious practices, but a few minutes or quiet time is surely needed by these children if we want them to grow as calm, composed, more complete, fulfilled individuals. We just cannot deny them of that need.

I can see no harm for students or children to believe in God. On the contrary, amazing things happen as evidenced by the life of a very bright student, Karen Cheng. Her name and picture was featured on the front page of a local newspaper on March 1996 saying, "Star student passes for being the best," She was declared as possibly the brightest high school student in the nation being a straight-A student with a perfect score on both the Scholastic Achievement Tests and the University of California acceptance index. Nobody had ever scored perfect on both before. I met with her, congratulated her, and asked if she can review my manuscript. She accepted. Her inputs to my book 'Today's S.O.S.' were valuable because her comments were not only intelligent, but also meaningful. It may interest you that her main comment was, *"I was interested to find that the book deals with God also. Bring in God throughout the book, because God fills every part of a believer's life."* That is not only intelligent, that is wisdom! Again, this is not about the religion or being religious. It is the personal relationship with God that makes a person complete, a big difference in one's life. Do we really want our children to be successful in all aspects of their lives? Simply take the formula from Karen. It works!

Do we really want the best for our children? Do we want a more positive change in our society and a better harmony in our environment? It is not just our children at school or the students at colleges and universities who need to connect with someone bigger and better than them, but WE ALL do. Us parents, teachers, church, school, government, and community leaders are likely needed prayers more as we face the demands of our daily responsibilities wherever we are. With so many problems we already have in our society, may these old phrases be a good reminder: *The fear (reverence) of the Lord is the beginning of wisdom.*

The family that prays together stays together.

Chapter 5

Yes! You Can Be Successful and Victorious!

Life is not all about money or making money.

*W*hy is it important for you to be healthy in all aspects of life? Because your means of SURVIVAL, SUCCESS and VICTORY in LIFE depend most on your *total well-being.*

Let's talk about SUCCESS. Is it something you have to strive hard for? If you are in a *healthy state of being,* that alone is already a success in itself.

SUCCESS or VICTORY - What's The Difference?

America - the land of milk and honey; the land of opportunity, where the citizens and immigrants are *success-oriented*. Go for the gold! Go for it! Success is in your hands. Success is everything, etc. All these true stories and (Beware!) seminars with all the hype and rallies packaged with books and tapes to buy to help you succeed. I will not discourage you from attending those because, personally, they helped me learn a great deal.

You see I saw both sides of the coin, both sides of their stories, the facts, the realities and fantasies. I learned that according to statistics, at least half of the attended would be excited and want to go for it. Picture this: Say you are attending a seminar with me. About half of that half will buy whatever is being sold. Others will not buy because they feel they don't need them; they can figure it out on their own; they are still skeptical; or they simply don't have the money at that time. Then out of those people, some will simply forget the whole thing when they wake up the next day, back to reality. Some, due to personal circumstances and other inhibiting factors will decide to just forget it. The truth is, less than one-tenth of those originally motivated people will actually do it. At the end, those who will make it or achieve their goal will be less than five percent (5%) of the motivated ones or only about one percent (1%) of those who first attended. Incredible!

No wonder why those who make it are branded as *achievers, winners*, and *successful*, feel elated, proud, on top of the world. The celebration begins, and continues... until the celebration is over. Then reality sets in... Are you happy? The question is, "How sweet is this success? How long will it last? What is true success?"

Observe the people around you, those you consider successful. Why do you consider them one, your 'measure of success'? Do they look happy, really happy? Let's visit some of these rich people, celebrities, lucky people who supposed to have everything. There was an American idol, who, long after he died, is still being idolized. He had great looks, a great voice, fortune and fame, but he ended up lonely and it is said that drugs caused his death. The same is true with the one who until now is considered the most beautiful woman who ever existed. Supposedly a successful, perfect life for both, but she ended the same way, lonely and on drugs. What else could they have asked for? Same questions are being asked on the cases of still living young celebrities. What could they be missing?

We continue to see famous figures in the society pages, in the movies, in sports, in business, even in politics – divorce, drugs, suicide, the rise and fall of so and so… What is going on? These people were certainly not average and ordinary. They have brains, talents, and most have worked hard to get where they are. They achieved their goals and their dreams, often beyond their wildest dreams. They are supposed to have 'perfect lives.' They are supposed to be happy!!! What is happening? Does this mean success does not guarantee happiness?

Let's face it. What are we missing here? Are these talks about success all lies? Somewhere, somehow, someone has been cheating us all along about what *true success* is. Those tragic events were not supposed to be the ending of those great stories, great people.

I believe it is time to come to our senses and evaluate what we are really striving for. Through my continuous search, I know that success is real. I have found people who are not only have achieved success, but who are also truly happy! Some are not necessarily rich and famous, but are happy and fulfilled. WOW, that's what we want, isn't it? Let's dig further and see if we are on the same boat with these folks. They said to first check your perception of success (meaning, not only what our society dictates to us, but your own measure of success). Is it a big house, nice cars, valuable and expensive possessions, high position, fame, power? Get a pen at this point and write your answer below (or on another piece of paper) and see what you come up with. Realize that because of our uniqueness to each other, the answers could vary greatly from each other. It doesn't matter. There is no right or wrong answer here because you are defining your own values. Now, what is your measure of success?

Second, evaluate whether those are really the most important things to you. How long will they last, or will you last when they are gone? Do the things you are striving for match those that are really important to you?

It is worth sharing what I have learned from a very happy man in our neighborhood. I respected him for his wisdom and always remembered what he said, and would like to pass on to you the message: He said, "The problem is, we allow ourselves to focus more on superficial successes (referring to material possessions, riches, power, fame, etc.) that fade away, disappear or vanish in time. It is the same with the excitement and happiness that they bring. We forget what's really valuable to us and those that has lasting value." Asked what he meant, he added, "Instead of riches, simply seek *to be your best* at all times. Instead of power, seek *health* and *peace*. Instead of fame, seek to *love* and be loved. Instead of seeking out the matters of this world, *seek God*, He is the source of life, the only true source of an abundant, meaningful, joyful and victorious life. All these will automatically bring you genuine, long lasting success and happiness." In conclusion, we both agreed that "When you are healthy, you are happy. When you are happy, it is easier to love and be loved. When you have all that, that is true success which no one can take away from you."

As we go through life, each one of us goes through the following STAGES. I found no one yet exempted, not even the royalty, the stars, the rich and powerful... no one so far:

Success → Mistakes/Failures → Trials → Victory (or defeat)

Based on human experiences, *success* is a much desired one – simply because it is pleasurable and gratifying. It is a source of pride that feeds our ego, and letting you feel ahead of mankind's competition. You feel great! It is self-fulfilling, which brings self-glorification. Then, mistakes and failures still happen. Some trials may come – one after the other, sometimes all at the same time. The situations vary in types, timing, severity and duration, depending on the case. These are considered the *life's true tests*, which can either break or mold us. It could be our end, or a way to help us grow into better, more mature individuals. Life's tests are usually unwelcome simply because they are painful and agonizing. It breaks our ego and actually helps or forces us to be humble. This can be difficult to take, especially if we still want to linger on celebrating our 'success.' This is our Waterloo. Our coping ability and how we deal with or handle our trials will determine if we will lose or win in life's true battle.

If you win, then you will realize the true joy of victory. If you noticed I no longer call it just success, but VICTORY. What is the difference? *Success* is when you have achieved something – your goal or others expectation maybe; or 'you have arrived' as most people put it. *Victory* is when your true abilities are tested, crushed or humbled. You go against all odds, beaten. At times, you feel alone, possibly even humiliated. But you do not accept defeat. You go on, not wanting to give up. And just before your last breath, you realize that you just crossed the finish line. You survived. You WON the battle! And whether anyone knows or cares, it doesn't matter anymore. The real joy is there. There is peace and true victory.

As you go through this life's path, remember, you are not alone! With the knowledge and natural abilities you have, or still waiting to be realized, you know you can face life. That you can welcome success, survive tough times, run life's race with renewed faith in God to carry you through, and WIN the race to VICTORY!

"The man who does things makes mistakes, but he never makes the biggest mistake of all – doing nothing."
– Benjamin Franklin,
American Statesman & Scientist

Live with a Song in Your Hearth

Can you imagine what our world would be like without music, without a song to sing or to listen to? Surely, it would be a very dull world indeed!

Music is the art and science of combining the sounds of voices or instruments or both in a pleasing sequence or combination. It can be any pleasant sound or series of sounds, such as a bird song or the sound of flowing water, referred as music to the soul. A song is a musical composition for singing.

We listen to music just about everywhere we go, practically everyday. Without much realization of it, we can appreciate what music does for us. Music is a big part of our lives simply because of the way it affects us. Each of us has a 'favorite song' that we love to listen to. And anyone can sing along, not just gifted singers. Each one of us can sing! There are songs that can change our mood, make us cry, and make us remember important events or people. Music is amazingly powerful in moving people to take action or experience certain feelings. Have you ever noticed how the music and songs are carefully selected in the movies to fit particular scenes? There are music or songs that encourage people to exercise (physical); to stimulate romantic feelings or other emotions (emotional); to motivate a person to use his mental power and be more productive (mental); to feel closer to or be in the presence of God, especially in a church setting (spiritual); to appreciate the meaning of friendship and humanity (social), etc. That is why records and tapes sell so well because they appeal to our whole being. They help make our world more beautiful and more colorful.

Because of our individualities, there will always be differences in our personal preferences of music, and we should respect one another for that. However, be aware that there is also so-called 'music' that is more of a 'peculiar noise.' The creator or which may be expressing anger, hatred, frustration or even desperation that can readily be transmitted to and internalized by the unsuspecting listener. There is no telling of the effect it can do to that listener. If the listener cannot detach him or herself from the message of that peculiar sound, the result can be very dangerous. We can prevent further undesirable events by alerting parents, educators and responsible regulators to be aware and make effort to orient our children about the psychological process involved here.

Instead, let us create good music in our hearts. Be selective by listening to music and singers that express or reflect happiness, love, peace and friendship. Carry a good song to live by. Like a refreshing water or a fresh breeze, a good song or a soothing music brings healing, inspiration, encouragement, peace, reconciliation, team spirit, hope and amazing power to go on. Singing while working or driving creates wonders.

Do you have a song in your heart? Get a good one and keep singing it. You will be amazed of how it pleasantly wakes you up in the morning so you can start a wonderful day.

Live with a Motto

"Love conquers all" is a short phrase but remains as one of the greatest mottos ever. A motto like this one does not need much explanations, it pretty much explains the power in itself.

A *motto* is a short sentence or phrase adopted as a rule of conduct or as expressing the aims and ideals of an individual, a family, a group, a country or an institution. Simple, short phrases similar to the one above have influenced and inspired people for ages.

Mottos are widely used, and we are familiar with many of them. Our early government adopted one and even inscribed it on our currencies, "IN GOD WE TRUST." Families, friends, teams, and different groups share this motto, *"United we stand, divided we fall."* A school has this written on its wall, *"Knowledge is a terrible thing to waste."* Another one says, *"If there is a will, there is a way."* Hospitals may have this one as their motto, *"Patients first."* Stores and businesses have mottos like this: *"Customer first", "Customer satisfaction is our #1 policy."* In sports, you can frequently hear this one, *"The game is not over until it is over."* Regardless of your involvement or interest, many of us can still learn from each other's motto.

Probably the most widely used motto in sports and also for business is "Just DO IT!" A known sport merchandiser took it as their slogan and made "Just do it!" a household phrase and, together with known celebrities, helped Nike reach phenomenal growth and popularity. Mottos and phrases like these can be very powerful. When you hear a parent, a boss, or a leader say, "Don't just think about it or say it, DO IT!" seem enough to actually influence people to take action or do something.

Can you see how this powerful concept can be used to influence us individually and collectively? We can use it to adopt something we like which will help us grow and improve. We can even make up our own motto to live by.

In my case, I found a motto to be a natural part of my life. We use mottos a lot at home and at school. I found them to be very important. My personal mottos were mostly passed on by my father (though I never really tracked down where he got them or where they came from). Others I picked up from school and from other people. The mottos will most likely be passed on to my children as well. Let me share my favorites with you.

"Do to others what you want others do to you." Don't do to others what you don't want others do to you." This reminds me always to put myself in the other person's place and think, 'How I want to be treated is the way I should also treat this person.' Of course, I still goof once in a while, but I try my best and learn more from each incident. Overall, this motto has helped me a lot when dealing with others, including my dear husband and children.

"Do it right or don't do it at all." That means, give your best at all times or don't even bother if you cannot give your best. It also means do it if you know it is the right thing to do. If not, if you are in doubt, don't do it at all. Strong words from my father, but I like it. It makes a lot of sense to me.

"Say what you mean and mean what you say. Otherwise, why say it?" Is a very impressive phrase I got from a very remarkable lady, my Aunt Letty.

"Don't do tomorrow what you can do today." Simply, do not procrastinate. There are times when I relax and take it easy, thinking it will not hurt to postpone something, that I really need the break or to rest. Otherwise, if I can do it now why waste my time? Time is so valuable. It is one thing I cannot take back once it has passed. Utilizing my time wisely makes me more productive and useful. That adds to my feeling of fulfillment and happiness, of course. This motto reminds me each day to do as much as I can for the day. This is also where I learned to have a sense of urgency, to treat each of my day as if it is my last, so I ought to give my best each day.

"When one door closes, a better one is waiting for me." This is a great motto that will prevent us from being very disappointed or depressed when things didn't work out as we wanted to. Giving up will never be an option in order to survive tough times in life, because this motto will remind us that there are always brighter tomorrows, better opportunities.

Motto is a good *guide* to fruitful, meaningful living. It is like adding another valuable tool to your "backpack for living a good life in harmony with your universe."

America, there must have been a good reason for our forefathers to have chosen a motto for our country. We should not lose sight of it and always remember what had made AMERICA a very special and strong nation. It is a short motto, but a very powerful and meaningful one:

"IN GOD WE TRUST"

Live One Day At a Time - As If It Is Your Last

There are many people nowadays who are still tied up with the pains and heartaches of *yesterday*. This tends to affect their joy or in some way hinder their potential and productivity for today.

There are also people obsessed with working very hard for their future. How do you know if the *future* or *tomorrow* will even come? There is really nothing wrong with thinking and preparing for tomorrow, provided that whatever is needed TODAY is not being neglected.

I know of a man who loves his family very much. After his honeymoon, he started working very hard, day and night, with the intention of providing the best future for his wife and children. He became very successful in his career and made a lot of money. Along with that, he acquired more responsibilities. He missed his family, but he rationalized that he had to do it now while he was young so he could have more time with them later. After two years, his wife divorced him, taking their baby with her. She said she could not take it anymore, saying, "I could no longer continue living with a man who is married to his job." He was devastated, and felt like a total failure. He eventually neglected his job and business as if they didn't matter anymore.

Incidents like this one, especially for a family, are very sad to witness. Every day, we witness more and more situations like this, read about them in the newspaper, see them on TV. Some end results are devastating to the individuals involved, their community, even to our society. We continue to ask the question, "Could such situation be avoided or worked out?"

In my personal life, my married life included, I have experienced plenty of trials and learning situations to be able to fully appreciate how important it is to live ONE DAY AT A TIME. I have learned, as others eventually learn also, that I cannot set aside or neglect what is important today for the sake of tomorrow, a tomorrow that I am not even sure will really be there.

Does that mean I can now forget about my goals, dreams and aspirations for the future? Not really. Learning to *live one day at a time* simply means that as we consider our future, it is equally important to learn to focus on *giving and doing our best* TODAY, knowing that our effort today will also greatly and positively affect our future. *Giving and doing our best* means, not just focusing on one area of our life (like our job or making money) but also giving equal time and attention to things that are just as important (or maybe even more important), like family and your health. Remembering the six parts of our being, that means not neglecting or disregarding our physical well-being, eating right, rest and relaxation, for what good is your success if you become seriously ill? Remembering our loved ones, what good is your big house with everything in it if you do not have the people you care about to share it with? Remembering our fellowship with our Creator, what good are all these things if you lose your relationship with the One who gave it all to you and who truly loves you more than anybody else? And so forth, and so on. It is never too late to evaluate how you are spending your days and make a correction or modification to your life as necessary.

It is like the builder of a house. First of all, he has a plan. In that plan is the whole picture of what to accomplish (considering the future). He will not start at the end, putting on the paint and finishing touches; or not even in the middle, worrying about the type of walls or kitchen counter. He will not just concentrate on the living room or the kitchen, but will carefully consider the quality of work for every area of the house. He also knows he has to consider the needs and inputs of everyone who will be living in the house. He then plans what to do on a day-to-day basis, according to step by step priorities. Obviously, the first step, the first day on the site, is to concentrate on *building a strong foundation* (like in marriage). Once that is accomplished, each day that follows will be much smoother. Involvement of others at every step can also make a difference, remembering that people really prefer that we do it *with* them and not just for them.

Come to think that life here in earth is too short, it will be wise then to live each day to the fullest, make the most out of it. Don't wait for tomorrow what you can do today, like forgive or ask forgiveness; actually say "I love you!" to someone you love besides just showing it. Give flowers now not when it can't even be seen or smelled anymore.

Each day is a new beginning. We should focus on *giving and doing the best we know how.* Then, if tomorrow will be there for us, we will find *that the good things we did yesterday apparently would automatically take care of our tomorrow also.* And at the end of the day, after you've given your all, don't worry about what else you're not able to do. I see much wisdom on what A.L.Williams said in his book with the same title, *"All you can do is all you can do, and all you can do is enough."* This also reminds me of a bumper sticker with a smiling face that says, *"Don't worry, be happy!"* After today, a new day will come.

I remember a speaker in a seminar saying, "You want to have a good future? Learn to live each day as if it is your last. Give your very best to yourself, to your loved ones, and to others TODAY."

> *"If we did all the things we are capable of doing,*
> *we would truly astound ourselves."*
> – Thomas Edison, American Inventor

Chapter 6

If Life Is A Game,
Will You Lose or Win?

Life is a journey. Each life is a story.
Collectively, we make a history.

The Key to Success in Life

Time is gold. Health is wealth. Knowledge is treasure.

*Y*ou see how the tens of thousand dollars I spent to buy all the books and tapes, attend all these expensive seminars, all paid off well in value of I believe hundred times over. My husband used to say, "You are crazy, spending all these money for what? You could be buying other important *things.*" For me, he is referring to things that don't last or depreciate in value instead of appreciating. Now, he understands and agrees with me, it is what you call 'investment'. And the best investment we can make is to INVEST in YOUR SELF first, to gain more knowledge and personal development. When you know 'you know', you gain more confidence. That confidence allows you to be more comfortable to make decisions. That decision will spring you into action, which brings you closer to your vision or the things you really want to do and achieve in life. Focus not just on financial, but consider your total well-being.

There is a fine line between 'winning' and 'losing,' it is the way you THINK, YOU DECIDE.

Losing	**Winning**
It's not possible, I quit	I believe
I can't	I can
I may, I'll see if..	I will
Do nothing	Press on, make it happen

Damaging Unhealthy Emotions/Feelings: Hate, Fear, Worry, Greed, Jealousy, Unforgiving, Resentful, Bitter, Burned out.

Living Healthy Emotions/Feelings: Love, Joy, Peace, Understanding, Giving, Forgiving

All these are considered normal emotions, something that naturally come to each human being as a sudden feeling, a spurt of the moment. What you do after that few minutes is what matters. For the living emotions, you may hold on to them as long as you want because they are healthy to your whole being. You have to more aware of the damaging emotions as they come because they are dangerous to your total health and well-being, like cancer cells. These need to be put in control as soon as you recognize it is coming to you. Shake them off. Take some deep breaths. Switch back to the living emotions ASAP.

Disabling/Damaging Words and Thoughts: cursing, profanity, words that should not be expressed and cannot be written in this book.

Power Living Words and Thoughts: Wonderful! Awesome! Amazing! Marvelous! Terrific! Fantastic! Super! Great! Love, Joy, Faith, Believe, Peace, Hope, Prosperity. If what you are expressing is a living word (healing, healthy), GO SAY IT! *"I love you." "I forgive you." "You can do it!" "You're a STAR!" "I believe in you."* These are the thoughts that should fill your mind more and what should be spoken more to others, especially our children. It will make a huge difference to you and everyone around you.

People spend or waste more time and energy thinking why it can't work, it can't be done, or why it can't happen. Rather, think of how it can work and how you can make it happen. The thing is, if something has to happen, it will happen with or without you. *"If it is to be, it's up to me."* If something has to change for the better, it will be up to YOU.

YOU can be TRANSFORMED if you want to.
It's your choice, your decision...

From: Wonderer	→	Spectator	→	Active Participant/Maker
Loser	→	Mediocre	→	Winner
Borrower	→	Owner	→	Investor/Multiplier
Poor	→	Middle Class	→	Wealthy/Abundant
Dependent/Taker	→	Self-sufficient	→	Financially Independent/Giver
Nobody	→	Average and Ordinary	→	Extraordinary
Miserable	→	Survivor	→	Victorious

In the Book of Life, you will find there that many supposedly hopeless people in the history were transformed because of faith or belief:

a blind from birth see; a bleeding woman healed; a lame walk; a captive free.

It is not what other people think or your horoscope say about you. The secret is in what YOU THINK and BELIEVE. The ultimate secret is YOU, in relations to *the One who lovingly created you.* You now just entered a new beginning, facing an unlimited universe and everything in it that are at your disposal for good reasons and purpose, for you to enjoy and to share with the world. Go ahead, create one and write down on your 'dream board' *"My Personal Dreams, Goals and Purpose"* for you to focus on each day you wake up. You may put it on your refrigerator or your favorite mirror or anywhere visible to you. Be specific. Put a target date. All you need now is to believe and take action or act on your belief. Walk each day carrying the faith in your heart. Go and make great things happen! Watch the sleeping giant in you wake up to the realization that you are meant to be a conqueror, finding your true treasures. Live and enjoy your life to the fullest, for the delight and honor of your Creator, your God, your Father.

The key to success in life, healthy, joyful, wealthy or abundant is already *in* you. TODAY is the time and the chance you have been waiting for. Don't let anything or anybody stop you now. GO FOR IT! Follow your dreams. The key to life success and victory is *within* you. Welcome home!!!

Key Points/Summary:

BELIEVE. The universe is more than happy to give you what you want – your dreams, your visions, your goals, your strong desires in life. You and the universe can only harmoniously make things happen when you are 'open', meaning you 'believe' that whatever good things that come to your mind is real, use your imagination as if it is already there, and you are simply taking the action (moved by your belief) that are necessary to make things happen. When you believe, you spring into action, thus will make what you believe a reality, together with the people and event set up by the universe towards your path as a result of the 'harmony' or 'connection' you created with the universe with your belief. When you are 'close' or do not believe or stopped believing, that immediately shuts off or disconnect the flow of what the universe can help you supposedly accomplish. Remember, if what you are thinking is something good, it is just a matter of YES or WAIT. It is only 'no' when you stop believing or if the outcome will not be good for you. Of course, the universe will not stop you when you insist your way anyway, just know that there are corresponding consequences to our own actions. Predictable results – you already know that what you expect /believe is what will happen. Guard your mind of what it believes because that is what will happen.

THINK BIG. It does not matter what your dream or goal is, BIG or small, when you believe, it will happen, and that is exactly what you will get. So, if the dream that came to you seem to be huge or impossible, believe it anyway and GO FOR IT! Remember, it is not called miracle if it is easy to achieve. It is called so because it is supposed to be 'impossible', that is why 'Mission Impossible' clicks. So, what do you have to lose? DREAM BIG! BELIEVE! And GO FOR IT!

Be of COURAGE. There is 'good' and 'evil' side on each story, book, play or movie. The villains are real in our true life. The universe is designed or created for the good, for our good. The evil thoughts, desires, and results that only leads to loss, violent death or destruction brought by the people influenced by or allowed themselves to be subjected to the evil doings. Once you realize and made a decision that that is not what you want in your life, believe that you have the power in you to resist the evil, to decline or reject the destructive suggestions. You will learn to discern, the ability to distinguish from right or wrong, from good or evil thoughts, feelings or actions. This is where we truly need God in us, the good spirit in us, His Spirit in you, because in time of human weakness, He can make us strong, victorious. What do you believe?

TAKE ACTION. Did you listen to Mark and Earl's message? If you did, GREAT JOB! If not, or you haven't heard of it ever, then do yourself a big favor, go in front of your computer, and listen. If you really want to achieve something great for yourself, you got to TAKE ACTION! Gaining information alone is not good enough. Knowledge alone without the application or action results to 'nothing.' You have to develop the habit of actually putting the knowledge or gathered information into ACTION. Action creates RESULT. Good, constructive ACTION produces productive REACTION or result (applying the CAUSE and EFFECT principle). You also need to translate your BELIEFS into ACTION. Make things happen. You, too, can be a MOUNTAIN MOVER, an IMPOSSIBILITY ACHIEVER!

GIVE. *'It is when you give that you receive, and the more you give the more you will receive.'* This does not only apply to money. You can give or share time, talent, ability, skill and or other resources. There is no small or insignificant piece in the game of completing the puzzle. Giving is like planting SEEDS. We can only expect a good harvest or result when we plant good seeds, our contribution to this great universe of ours. It is an amazing miracle that one small seed, like a mustard, a corn, an orange and so forth, which are too small or can seem insignificant, but when planted and nurtured (given faith), can grow to huge plants or giant trees to provide great produce, beauty, shade, home to birds, etc, enough to help create and contribute to our beautiful world. Let us give, contribute our part. Find your seed, plant them, nurture them and we will gladly watch with you as you make them flourish and be productive.

GROW and MULTIPLY. You are meant to be fruitful, productive, to grow and multiply, become an extension of God's blessings to others. Like a seed that is meant to be planted and nurtured so it can produce fruits. Then, you have something to share for others to enjoy. Just like the leading character in a great movie that, against all odds and adversities, at the end will come out triumphant or victorious, bringing not only great entertainment to the viewers, but most likely a great inspiration to many who needed just that boost to help them go on in life, to dream and believe again. To believe one more time that he, too, can do it. It can happen to him, too. As you exercise this principle, then the more you will appreciate the concept of the Power of Duplication and Multiplication.

Be HAPPY, REJOICING always! Be positive. Have fun. Laugh. We are in this big world together, whether you like it or not, we will affect one another. We might as well *"work-together"* for common good, for everybody's sake. Shall we? My husband and children occasionally remind me, "Mom, when you're not happy, we're not happy. When you are happy, we're all happy." Take notice of how the people around you at home, work or anywhere else are when you are happy or grouchy. They are but reacting or responding to the vibration you are sending. (Remember the mirror?) As the old saying goes, *"SMILE, and the world will smile back to you."*

Find a reason to be happy always. When you are *happy,* you bring *health* to yourself. When you are *healthy*, which makes *you appreciative and happy*, a cycle that will keep revolving to your life if you determine to do so. The best part is, at that state of your being that you become more a *'magnet'* to good things in life (Law of Attraction). Learn to reject unhappy thoughts and suggestions, its unhealthy, nonproductive.

What I loved about the popular Disney movie 'The Lion King' is its profound message: In spite of all difficulties and challenges, *Hakuna Matata*. Don't worry, be HAPPY!!!

Remember, the true living and loving God in you always. The Book of Life talks clearly about this subject, *"Don't worry about anything. Instead pray for everything." "REJOICE always!"*

> *"Action is the antidote to despair."*
> — Juan Baez, American Folk

> *"One of the greatest of all principles is that men can do what they think they can do."*
> — Norman Vincent Peale

Today's Tough Questions, Tough Issues

Have you ever asked yourself this question:

> *"Despite of vast resource for information, modern technology, well-funded research and projects, medical advancement and others that supposed to make our life better, how come we now face the worst health, economic and environmental crisis?"*

For sure I am not the only one who has many questions, that need answers… and possible solutions.

Though it varies, we confront many life challenges today that we need to deal with. The BIGGEST and most CRITICAL CONCERNS and ISSUES we individually and collectively face are:

- **Health and Wellness Concerns**
- **Economic or Financial Concerns**
- **Environmental, Climate and Weather Concerns**
- **Relationship Concerns and Human Behavior Issues**
- **And more…**

To deal with these challenges and issues present in our time, to see them for what they really are, to do something about it, it is best to

125

make a determination if it's either a FALLACY, FACT or REALITY. Let's have a clear understanding of the terms, according to our dictionaries:

Fallacies – a mistaken belief, misconception, faulty reasoning, misleading or unsound argument.

Facts – reality, actuality, certainty, something known to exist or to have happened; something known to be true. The quality or state of being actual or TRUE.

Realities – includes everything that is and has been, whether or not it is observable or comprehensible.

The TRUTH became so debatable nowadays, depending on the eyes of the beholder or opinion of people. The truth is truth that cannot be contested. But again, we are in a society where the truth doesn't matter much anymore, as long as it caters to individual arguments of what's right or wrong... according to their opinion or people's insistence of their right to make a choice... based on convenience or what they feel will benefit them. The truth became such a gray area to some, which created more confusion and uncertainties to people, especially to our young ones. We have witnessed truth to be twisted to different forms. So we will leave *the truth* to be the responsibility, and for accountability purposes, of the readers. You get to make up your mind, truth or not.

For example. When we hear the saying, *"When you have plenty of money, you have many friends. When you don't have money, you are out of friends."* This can be closed to truth, but not a matter of fact. People tend to make this statement based on their personal experiences, which may vary. During conversations, the listeners then tend to agree or disagree, again based on their own experiences and situations. Each make their own conclusion, whether this statement is a fallacy, a matter of fact or reality. In our current society, the TRUTH, or not, becomes debatable.

This in fact is one huge reality we face in our modern society. Seeking the truth comes secondary to what or how the opinion or situation favors the person, group or company's stand or profit margin. Sooner or later, we have to ask, *"Is this selective process really favorable for the individual or collective short-term outcome? How about long-term?"*

> *"Darkness cannot drive out darkness; only light can do that. Hate cannot drive out hate; only love can do that."*
>
> – Martin Luther King Jr.

Together, let us **spread the Message of HOPE, LOVE, HARMONY and VICTORY!**

As a practicing professional in the fields of Health, Finance and Business, my practical principles and conclusions are naturally based on *science, logic and simple common sense.* We can begin with the cause or root. Facing the truth and realities can help us reach real solutions.

Roots of Today's Problems:

- Too much politics and "politically-correct" self-serving principles and practices.
- Too many man-made religion and church-focused activities, rules and traditions, yet lack of action or practice of what is necessary to maintain community wellness and human dignity among people.
- Complacency. No urgency to take action on things not necessarily affecting self.
- Displaced way of expressing love. Love "self" more than love of others.

Through the years, as a community health advocate, educator and volunteer, I relentlessly advocated a *Total Wellness* approach to creating abundance in all areas of our life: physical, mental, emotional, spiritual, social and even financial. Being in the *Healthy Zone* as an individual, and working collaboratively with your community, is highly encouraged for everyone's wellness or good.

As individuals, and as a community, let's freely talk about these things. Social media became popular because of the need for venue where people can freely communicate.

On top of our list, Health and Wellness Concerns and Issues are much integrated and greatly affect the Financial and other Concerns and Issues. Nowadays though, more people are stressing out about their finances, as they rationale that their HEALTH and HAPPINESS, if they want to be, are much dependent on their FINANCIAL FREEDOM or security (meeting the needs, and wants). Because of that, though I believe more on putting priority to our *health*, it is also a fact that *financial wellness* is very much a part of our *total well-being*. So let's begin…

Economic or Financial Concerns and Issues:

Economic Crisis – How can a country, like America, fix its still rapidly growing national debt in now tens of trillions of dollars? What can you expect from leaders who don't seem to know how to balance the budget? How did they get in their positions in the first place? Do they really intend to make things right? If our eyes are open, we can see and find out that:

> ➢ Millions of qualified laborers are unemployed, underemployed, or have to work two or three jobs just to make ends meet. The opportunity available for our today's graduates is slim. I've met graduates who are dismayed for being unemployed, some homeless.
> ➢ Good hard-working people driven from their homes are now part of the staggering number of homeless. These are not

just individuals and adults, many are families with young children.

➢ Too many can no longer afford decent meals or nutritious food.

➢ Dependency or entitlement mentality among many keeps growing in an alarming rate. This includes our youth (as if it is a generational privilege). This cripples our nation's budget. This system robs our adults and youth of their true dignity and potential. We need to become individually concern and take collective action, if we want to prevent America's progression into a third world country?

Here is a brief overview of the situations we currently face individually and as a society. These challenges affect all of us, and call for everyone to seek and contribute for immediate solutions.

FINANCIAL and RETIREMENT ISSUES:

Are you ready to RETIRE? If you are a Senior or approaching retirement, then you are most likely already aware of the problem the baby boomers are facing right now. Are you aware of the report below released by the US Department of Labor? I first learned of this during the '80s. Over thirty years ago it was like this, and it is not getting any better but worse. I am just amazed how many seniors are neither aware nor prepared for this impending predicament:

> *"Today, of every 100 people who reach age 65, only 2 are financially independent, 23 must continue working, and 75 must depend on friends, charity, or relatives. Of every 100 Americans reaching age 65 today, a horrifying 96 are flat broke."*
>
> – U.S. Department of Labor (1980s)

I thought things will get better, but not only that the retirement age is delayed to 67, I am seeing the reality with more seniors continuously working to supplement their income. Will you be financially secure, dependent on others, or will you continue to work throughout your life?

In an October 2005 issue of TIME Magazine, a front page headline reads, *"The Great Retirement Rip Off – Millions of Americans who think they will retire with benefits are in for a nasty surprise... TIME magazine investigates why the Golden Years are in peril."* The article features pictures of seniors, one collecting cans and another still working at age 78, just to supplement their income and pay medical bills.

Can the course of the financial crisis taking place in America, and in some respects around the globe, be changed? The answer is, YES!

The 'DEPENDENCY' or 'ENTITLEMENT' MENTALITY Issue:

Findings show that the segment of our population that does not make enough money to meet their basic needs is growing alarmingly. That is true, but at the same time there are just too many people depending on our government to supply for their basic existence or supplement their income so that they may live and pay for their medical needs. Those with disabilities, who are truly unable to work, and our seniors, who fairly made their contributions, are well justified expecting the government to fulfill its promises. More alarming is our population's younger generation, who has joined the 'generations of dependents' in our society, called the WELFARE system. This is becoming a huge burden because the individuals are not able to function as healthy and productive members of our society. Is it possible to affect a change on people's dependent tendencies? The answer is, YES!

As my family and I experienced the economic downfall as the result of real estate bubbles (and its underlying roots) starting in the late 1990s, the financial deterioration for individuals, the massive foreclosures and lay-offs were watched in horror by many in our nation. Most of the time unable to figure out what's going on, especially when things are happening too fast beyond what they can begin to comprehend. The financial, mortgage and credit deterioration extended to other investing countries. It got so bad that it turned into a *global economic crisis*. To date of the completion of this book, America and many other countries are still scrambling for solutions. Years had passed and still people wonder if our leaders could really come up with answers to reverse the widely spreading spiral effect of the disasters and calamities mankind created and now face.

At this point of time which already created a significant mark in human history, many millions of people in the US and around the globe lost their jobs, their homes and some even felt had lost their human dignity. Many seniors who felt they've worked so hard to secure their retirement, now feel betrayed that they lost their equities and now facing financial insecurities. We also cannot neglect to consider our children and future children who will inherit too much debt which experts already predict they may not be able to pay in their lifetime. It is normal or expected for people to ask, "How could all this happen?" or "How could the people we trusted allow these things to happen?"

Discussions are acceptable. In fact, it should be encouraged to allow people to ventilate, express their feelings and thoughts. This process can bring some relief to at least the emotions they are experiencing. Expression is one thing. The most important that we should get out of this situation, so something good could come out from it, are:

1. Lessons that can be learned, individually and collectively.
2. Come up with solutions, individually and collectively.
3. Bring people back together as they implement the best plan of action they can come up with - for the sake of individuals, families, communities, and us all globally.

Now we got to ask the question, WHAT COMES NEXT?

Health and Wellness Concerns and Issues

It is quite interesting that while *malnutrition* is a great problem in other countries, in America, referred to as "the land of excess," the statistics show that OBESITY is of great concern for many people, including our youth. The health problems associated with obesity, including hypertension, diabetes and heart diseases have not only physical effect, but most often also mental, emotional, social and financial impact on the individuals with obesity problem. We can also add to these issues the *inadequate nutritional information* and *weight loss obsession*, especially among our younger generation, which caused EATING DISORDERS to become more prevalent. Incidentally, these health challenges also put huge financial burden on our already crippled government health-care system and budget. Are there solutions and preventive measures for these problems? The answer is, Yes!

Another socially related issue is how this also has great impact on the overall health of the entire family. There are more SEPARATED or DIVORCED couples than there are married couples staying together nowadays. Divorce puts physical and financial strain on the whole family, but more concern should be directed towards the mental and emotional impact on our children who are being exposed to unstable family environment. At times these children are ending up displaced or disassociated from much needed nurturing environment. Can more of these situations possibly be prevented? The answer is, Yes!

When Feeling Sick or Having a Check-Up - When you are feeling something is not right, afraid you may really be sick this time, you thought of seeing a doctor. That's normal. You make the doctor's appointment. The doctor see you for few minutes, ask few questions, told what tests will be done, then perhaps at that moment give you some prescription. I know, I've been there, seen that, as both a professional nurse and a patient.

Most patients would go home, relieved or more anxious, still not knowing exactly what the sickness is about, why feeling ill, and what the medication will do to help. All one could do is TRUST the Physician, after all he's a doctor. He should know what he/she is doing, right? Well, just letting you know that you are also entitled to think again, do some inquiries or do some research before you trust your life away. If you learn to listen to your own body, and learn how to keep yourself healthy and prevent or combat illnesses, you will surely know better what to do.

My best recommendation: ASK your Doctor QUESTIONS. Next, do your RESEARCH, especially if you were prescribed medications. Be aware of their side effects and other precautions. Make sure the benefits outweigh the accompanied risks. I recommend asking the doctor next time: *"What's wrong with me Doc? WHY am I sick?"* (And why people has to go through so much test to determine even slightest ailment. Some are unnecessary or can put more lives at risk.) Ask the *cause* or the *root of the problem*. Are you aware that, and has been proven, most diseases and illnesses has to do or caused by NUTRITIONAL DEFICIENCIES. Ask your doctor, see how much he/she knows about this subject, and possible real solution to your problem.

Next important question, after the doctor gives you a diagnosis: WHAT can help CORRECT or RESOLVE this problem, the real SOLUTION? How do I/we treat this problem so that I will no longer have hypertension, diabetes, cancer, be overweight or malnourished, etc. but be TOTALLY HEALTHY?

An interesting question was thrown at me: *"Do you think the doctors would really like us healthy?"* Why not? Think about it. If we're now all healthy, many will lose their job or practices. Hospitals will close their business! Many huge pharmaceuticals will lose their billion dollar annual profit. Hmmm... something to consider.

Again, do you know WHY you are sick or what makes you sick? If you go home from that doctor's visit, and all you got are prescriptions, and not told WHAT, WHY and HOW, then you failed to ask and receive real helpful answers.

Are there *alternatives* or *options*, like more *natural remedies* vs invasive procedures. *Holistic, integrated, chiropractic medicines* are becoming known or popular nowadays. Your regular modern doctor would like you to see these as "quack doctors," but are they? You will not know the answer to that, unless you ask and search for answers.

FAIR WORD of WARNING! Be careful on your search though. Check the source, check out several resources. It will not hurt to get referrals or references.

This may interest you. Do you know the average age of doctors dying? According to one doctor, Dr. Joel Wallach who authored *Dead Doctors Don't Lie* and has over fifty million books sold internationally, the average life span of doctors or MDs in America is 58! Whoo... I thought they knew how to be healthy? Come to realized that I personally have known and heard of doctors and even nurses who died early at their forties and fifties, by all kind of cases: cancer, health attack, stroke, etc.

The truth is, **the appointed time for us to be born and die on this earth: Only God knows.**

When your mother was pregnant with you, was she told by the obstetrician of your day of delivery. How accurate is it? According to studies, only less than 5% of birth with given due date actually happened on that day. So, forget about or don't stress out over this due date. It is still okay or expected to be born around two to three weeks prior or after the expected due date. Until now, doctors wonder why babies take their sweet time in coming out of this world.

Numerous situations and experiences tell me this "Health Enterprise System" is still a "hit or miss" scenario. Many patients are willing guinea pigs. You can be lucky, or not. The bill will still be the same.

Health Crisis – Instead of educating the public on *how to maintain health* and, thus, *prevent illnesses*, we are being bombarded daily with enticing advertisements about unhealthy food and world events that make us live with stress or fear. In spite of billions of dollars spent on so-called researches, instead of being a healthier nation, more people, including a growing number of youth and younger children, are taking the unhealthy path to diet. More are into prescriptions, or over-the-counter drugs. The latter issue is madness, as many experimental drugs floating out there are could have hidden dangerous side effects.

What Helped My Own Health Struggle:

I recommend the **preventive approach** in maintaining wellness. This is a much better health option. I urge you to take time to find out more. Don't allow your health to be compromised and simply dependent on prescription drugs or over-the-counter medicines. Invasive surgery is, likewise, something to really think about. Unfortunately, perhaps, for most patients, it is too late to realize that going *back to basics* with the true wisdom of *natural* remedies and healing processes could have been the healthier path to wellness. Why do you think many doctors don't take their own prescribed medicines? Go and read many good online information and publications about prevention as key to maintaining wellness. I find Suzanne Somers' books to be interesting literature on this area. They are rich with non-biased researches and testimonies. It is an eye opener. Some natural remedies she used helped me with my quest to true wellness.

Allow me to share with you here what helped me recover from my past health issues and regain my health to the point I'm everyday grateful. I have not felt this healthy my entire life! I did a lot of research online and offline, observed and interviewed a lot of healthy looking people. I searched for healthy lifestyle – less stress, fresher or cleaner air and water, more natural, organic, nutritious food. Being happy and grateful no matter what.

There are also supplements, immune boosting food and other helpful means I studied and tried myself, realizing there's just no way I can eat or produce all the wonderful supplements my body would prefer to have, on my own. I tried the noni, aloe, acai, mangosteen, malunggay or *moringa oleifera*, bitter melon, etc. I call them *superfood*.

While people are much discouraged by the negative comments or reviews on such natural remedies and supplements, when you decide you need it, you can only best trust your gut feeling or instinct of what ultimately may be best for you. Don't put that important decision on somebody else's hand. Surely I subjected myself as my own guinea pig on these products, after my due diligence of course. The result has been very satisfying. I am healthy at last! At this point, I am very grateful that I could declare I'm completely healthy in all areas. It feels so good to wake up each morning feeling so well. (Not all day, but just about.) I've never been this healthy and energized! (I've been very sickly as a child, and kept getting worse, I thought I would die before forty.)

During my health teachings, my attendees would ask where they can find the sources for true wellness. They ask for my secrets for health. I hesitated endorsing any product or company in the past, but how do I actually help people if I'll keep the information, or secrets, to myself? Now, taking my stand to truly serve, I would mention few here, as it could be helpful to those who are already searching for resources for better health. You have to do your due diligence though, and decide which will be best for you.

Yes, there are great companies out there I continue to order from for personal health maintenance: **Zeal** *by* **Zurvita** for their all-in-one formula; **Lifewave** for their marvel patches; **do Terra** for their wonderful natural essential oils various use; **Youngevity** with Dr Joel Wallach and his complete nutrition approach; a few **Nature's Pearl** and the muscadine grape, with the founder's amazing anti-cancer discoveries, just to name few... For sure there are more good products and companies out there waiting to be discovered.

I am particularly very excited about my latest discovery called **"ZEAL for Life"** by *Zurvita*. It lived up to its name. It is amazingly packed with all my favorite super food in one, plus more real good nutrients important to support my whole body system. Their simple small bottles with powder formula, simply mixed with water when ready, is a huge plus for me. It is so convenient especially when I am traveling. The affordable cost makes it a true winner! No longer can anyone say, *"I can't afford to be healthy."* Check it out, for your own healthy body.

I would say, be open-minded to research (you have to make your due diligence for your safety). Read as much, make inquiries or gather testimonies of people who have actually used them. Once you find which ones fit your health situation and wellness goal best, it will be worth your time and effort.

I would like to personally thank the wonderful men and women, and companies, who made the vital discoveries of the natural based products that helped me heal completely and enjoy true wellness again! Acknowledgement and great appreciation for the individual health and wellness practitioners, groups, organizations, for sharing, for your dedication and passion to bring to the public what's truly healthy. You are making a huge difference and I or WE want to say from the bottom of my heart, **"THANK YOU!"**

Environmental, Climate and Weather Concerns and Issues

Why do we have Environmental, Climate or Weather Problematic Changes?

When it reach the irreversible point, according to our scientists, what happens then?

How significant are the sun flares? NASA is watching this very closely as it could affect many infrastructures in our world today. What can be done? Also of concern is possible man-made means to actually disable even our national or global power and communication grid. If people will only be open to researching and learning, they could be more prepared, or have the brilliance to help.

Have you heard of the unusual things happening, not just locally but around the globe in the last several months and years alone of more earthquakes, hurricanes, typhoons, floods, tornados, severe or sudden droughts, millions of dead marine species, thousands of birds playing havoc in the sky or drop dead on the ground, unusual scenes in the sky, etc. etc. And what on earth are the CHEM TRAILS and GEOENGINEERING, HAARP, FEMA Consecration Camps, and so on... any truth to them? Amazingly, numerous resources, from written publications, the internet, even YouTube videos provide plenty of information pertaining to these. Just ask. Be diligent and know which are fallacies, and which are facts.

How would you know what's real or not, to distinguish between someone's creative imagination or the truth, unless you search? Many movies, videos and documentaries are out there. Beyond entertainment, should you know and be more prepared to protect yourself and your love ones?

A fair question to ask, *"Could God be involved in all of this?"* Could it be possible that this loving and merciful God is allowing havoc and disasters in nature to affect people? Didn't He created Heaven and Earth and was so pleased? (Meaning, it must be perfect then.)

Or could these calamities be also "man-made," caused by human actions? So why blame God if it is humankind's own doing?

If God has any involvement, it is to bring us into the light of who we are and His promise based on our actions.

> *"If my people who are called by my name will humble themselves, and pray and seek my face, and turn from their wicked ways, then I will hear from heaven, and will forgive their sin and heal their land."*
>
> – II Chronicles 7:14

Relationship Concerns and Human Behavior Issues

It is easier to write what readers would rather hear, but isn't it time to examine the facts and realities? Wouldn't it be better to face the TRUTH? How do we get to the truth when words such as lies, deceptions, cover ups, and so on, become the norm? These become more prevalent in a society which promotes "I, me and "myself" self-centeredness. As a result, selfishness, greed, power and control obsession grows. In reality, the roots of these are feelings of insecurity or emptiness, with underlying ignorance, arrogance or rebellion. Time will come when people would not distinguish anymore what is real or not, what is truth or not. There will be such confusion, it will be hard for people to determine whom to trust, or to still trust. Is this the kind of society we want to live in?

What about this subliminal or subconscious programming which gives effective suggestions to people's mind without them realizing it. This type of programming is why advertising works in selling products, ideas or ideology, to the unsuspecting population.

Based on human experiences, it is evident that real solutions are not dependent on the greatest wealth, power or position on earth. It is unfortunate when the highest political positions we allow to rule in power are there to possess, more than to serve. (There are exceptions, of course.) Many of those in power, knowingly or unknowingly, introduced more conflicts in this world by their "**politics**" and introducing the word "**politically correct**." Though well-worded, in the eyes of God, these are but *foolishness*. The name used alone clearly implies that.

Even the countless types of **religions**, **gods** (we have plenty of these), have not brought true peace. Interestingly, they have become the source of more discourse, disagreements, conflicts and wars.

All I know is that we have a little window of time to do what is right for all our sake. No one can do it all. It will take *each* of us, *all of us together*, to agree *to go back to the basic of true wellness* so we can experience true love and harmony. Families and communities need to come together, to determine to be there for one another, because time will come when none of the things we know of in this world will matter. We cannot bring any with us. No one can escape...

No matter what your opinion is, it is no brainer that *heaven is heaven, and hell is hell.* It is just a matter of choice, now and not later. I didn't have to include this part, but I care enough to tell it like it is. This most important decision you have to make will definitely affect the rest of your life in eternity. Again, only our body dies. Our immortal spirit goes on forever. Don't allow yourself to be influenced by others' opinion, because you and only you will be responsible for your decision.

If there is a way that can assure me of being transformed and belonging to this place called the **New Heaven and Earth** where there will be no more sickness, pain, tears or sorrow (or bills or taxes to pay), why would I take the risk not knowing where will I go next? Risking going someplace else? It doesn't make sense. That is the risk I don't dare take. If God wants to start all over again, and make sure it is going to be all perfect this time, I am definitely going with Him!

It made sense… This must be the reason why Jesus, the only known Son of the Living God, Who came to earth in form of human flesh, the One who shed His blood on the cross for the ransom of many. Yes, He died, yet on the third day rose again, seen by many. He ascended to heaven and joined God the Father. (And this by the way is not just a fictional story, but part of our history. It is a fact. It is the truth.) In His Word, He said…

> *"For God did not send His Son into the world to condemn the world, but that the world through Him might be saved."*
>
> – John 3: 17

> *For God so loved the world that he gave His only begotten Son, that whoever believes in Him should not perish but have everlasting life."*
>
> – John 3:16

Many who belong to certain religions worship all kinds of idols, small 'gods' including 'self.' It is important to be able to have a *personal relationship* with the true LIVING GOD by simply believing and receiving Him into your life. That's what happened to me when I was in college. I received Jesus in my heart, and to this day can attest that it is the best decision I have done in my entire life. Through all these years I learned, in spite of all knowledge, science, logic, success and sophistication, life remains full of tests, trials and tribulations. Without a *personal relationship* with God who is the source of strength and true solutions, life can be too tough for anyone to handle. He is real and truly loves us. All needed is believe and receive Him in your life as your personal Lord and Savior. That's all. No rituals. No traditional process. Less rules… only to *love God* and to *love one another.*

141

GREATEST DISASTER OF ALL TIME:

I believe however, that the greatest disaster of all time is that there are **people who have lived their lives without even knowing their potentials.** Sad to say, many people nowadays merely EXIST, *rather than* LIVING. Can this be corrected or improved? The answer is, YES!

YES! The GOOD NEWS is: LIFE can still be different, exciting and meaningful! It can still be better for all of us. Don't let anything or anyone stop you on your road to discovery. Don't let any negative thoughts tell you that you can't, that it is impossible...because YOU CAN! And ANYTHING is POSSIBLE!

What about the WARS? Why do we have wars? Who needs or wants it? Who are really benefiting from wars? How is the war benefiting anyone, if there's any benefit at all?

While we express our deepest gratitude to our brave men and women who obeyed and paid the ultimate sacrifices to give us our freedom, along with their families who made their painful sacrifices with them, believing they are depending their families and citizens of their countries... But then we have to ask questions: For who? Really for WHO, or for WHAT?

We know that in war, there will always be casualties. Don't need to give statistics here. We see the news just about every day, and it changes or accelerate each day. We are grieved with sadness. Then, people become callous as it becomes a daily occurrence, as if it's just now a normal part of life. Is it?

This really mind-boggle me. Anything good that resulted from previous and current wars? Please enlighten me, as I've given this subject full consideration, made my researches, and still remain unconvinced that something good actually comes from war. Is whatever our veterans fighting for really worth the price paid?

Consider the expenses that we've been hearing for a long time hurting our federal budget, that could been used more productively; the tragedies and displacements faced by families, on both sides. Do we have anyone at all who can testify to the biggest gains and victories compared to the biggest losses of lives and properties and other devastating results of these wars?

So WHY keep doing it? Shouldn't we ASK these fair QUESTIONS? Are we just going to continue to watch the effect, the results of war… again FOR WHAT or FOR WHO really?

I was finishing writing on this topic when I read on the internet news the announcement that Congress approved *more Billions* to prevent the government from shutting down, increase the debt ceiling, once again. More shocking, that the budget is equally divided between domestic use and defense budget. The news says the House of Representative in November 2015 passed $585 Billion Defense Budget for 2015-2016. Is this for them the solution? Aren't this only creating more problems compounding to more or worse situation to the nationals, affecting entire humanity? We already witnesses this over the past years. May I ask, did the previous billions spent made our country any safer, secure or healthier?

Chills ran to my spine, as I thought, "This is insane!" That sounds like creating more monstrous weapons for more mass destruction. I'm still dumb pounded on how this suppose "to protect"? …that the government actually put such priority on weapons and wars vs building means to improve people's wellbeing.

Do you know by the way, that this bill will add $3 copay to military health benefits while other benefits are reduced for troops and their families? This alone makes me ask, how could this be for the better? Also, if this budget is from borrowed money, how do these government leaders' plan to repay it?

Imagine using such amount to improve the quality of lives of people, locally and extended as necessary to our neighbors. Not on more useless and destructive weapons, but improving human lives by more practical daily living skills: education, ways to produce more natural nutritious food, and creating means to improve the quality of life of people. The results will be healthier and happier people everywhere. Instead of sad and horrifying news, we can then fill our environment with more good news! Positive, healthy actions produce more productive or fruitful results. Do these wealthy leaders don't feel any discomfort at all that they lost senses on what the little people's actual needs?

But then, who am I. Who will pay attention to this little and unknown individual at all?

Do we "little people" or the masses, truly have NO VOICE over few powers who run everything according to their wishes, with or without the knowledge or permission of THE PEOPLE? Something very wrong is going on, and the "little people" are just going to watch and grieve with the results and painful consequences of this irresponsible actions of leaders; and equally, the inattentiveness or inaction on the part of THE PEOPLE.

What is to happen is to happen. Each has to BE PREPARED, the only logical thing to do.

Could there really be PEACE?

Experience tells us that we cannot just depend solely on powerful world leaders to fix things for us, including maintaining peace and harmony in our world. Billions of dollars are being spent just talking about peace. On the surface it seems to be, for a little while. But in reality there's still so much disagreement, argument, distrust and, worse, continuous wars. World leadership of all time has created more havoc and disaster hard to fathom. Many supposedly leaders prove to be weak in truly serving their people. They desire to be served instead of the one to serve. Many agree that we have *enough* of conflicts and wars, causing only pain, destruction and sorrow.

144

There are no winners in these war games except those who sell and trade of arms. We are to take our individual responsibility to create and bring peace with our neighbors, and care for everyone.

Could it be that going back to God our Creator, the true Living God who breathes Life (the source of Aloha, the living Breath or the Life Himself) be our only hope? Is it really that difficult to follow His two basic instructions (as if the original ten commandments are too much to remember): *"Love God with all our being"* (meaning, complete surrender to Him), and *"Love others as you love yourself"* (or to love one another). Have we given it a real good effort? ...test how it works, or is it easier to just ignore or disregard these two ...at our own peril.

You and I can be at peace, with joy in our hearts, with thanksgiving and praise for the One who is the Beginning and the end of Life, the One who has the promise of eternal life in the coming New Heaven and Earth.

If this NWO (New World Order) is true, and that is for everyone to one day determine, then have no fear. Over five years ago, during one of my online researches, I encountered an interesting blog from those who watch what's happening in the world and what they share. It was interesting to note the open exchange of information and insights of folks from various parts of the world. One in particular caught my curiosity. The blogger said that words can be coined from the letters NWO, which he volunteered to provide: OWN NOW, which is supposedly the intent of a certain elite group. (At that time I didn't have the slightest clue of what he was referring to.) He added that an "antidote" is needed to combat their plan. Being in the health field, I was familiar with that term. This surely caught my interest enough to do further research. I was amazed from the vast information regarding this certain group and other related names and topics. To most people, this is something that can be frightful, or something that can easily be brushed off as something not real or manipulated idea. People will be tested in their judgment, reaction and action, wise or foolish it may be.

This was becoming like an adventure to me. Determined to find a solution or best course of action to this "antidote," I asked the

Almighty God who knows it all to help me. I was astonished with the answer! It is so relevant and appropriate: WON.

I got it! From then on, in spite of what I may hear or see happening, I know in my heart that I can have peace. Yes, the battle was already WON on the cross over two thousand years ago. We may not be able to stop these big global powers with their plans to OWN NOW, in whatever shape or form they will accomplish this, but they will never win this game. It is because the antidote belongs to true Living God alone. He is the only One who ultimately can claim the Victory. Before the Battle even begins, He, JESUS, YESHUA, the King of kings and the Lord of lords already WON the VICTORY!

What to do then in place of prevalent stress, worries and fears in our environment today? Be on the winning side with God, stay on the Healthy Zone. No matter what happens, when it happens, it will not affect you much anymore. Focus on spending your precious time and energy on things of value than merely existing or working for money.

Focus on investing more of your time and resources in *building your relationship with...*

> **#1 God**
> **#2 Family and dear Friends, and**
> **#3 Community or Others as Extended Family.**

This way, you can enjoy LIFE more fully, with peace, joy and fulfillment.

Let's celebrate LIFE! I see a good LIFE with...

> **L** – Love (caring, sharing)
> **I** – Integration, Interconnection
> **F** – Fulfillment of Purpose
> **E** – Empowered SO (Self and Others)

How about DEATH? The realities explains why there are those given death-sentence type diagnosis just somehow continue to live, and at some cases even totally recover! It is equally shocking when still young, healthy individuals suddenly dead – mostly due to vehicular accidents, homicide, or sudden illness. Is there any point to worrying?

Aim to live healthy and stay healthy, our best defense. *Preventive* is better and less costly than curative. Your body's time will come to conclusion. May it find you at peace and ready.

Now, let's talk about that... ARE YOU READY, anytime?

Life on Earth is short, represented by our physical body, which expires. There's eternal life, or death, which is very, very long or no ending. The fact is, only our BODY dies, which eventually, like it or not, will pass away. Our SPIRIT is IMMORTAL though, or no ending.

Question: Where your spirit will spend eternity?

Chapter 7

The Last Chapter

The best and most beautiful things in this world cannot be seen or even heard, but must be felt with the heart.

— Helen Keller

A Shared Vision

I found out that I am not alone in my vision, that it is being shared in various ways by many. The vision of *equal opportunity* and *abundance for all* citizens was shared by our American forefathers. Abraham

Lincoln and Martin Luther King are just two of many great people who shared the same vision for all the people in America. Today, I am seeing that those dreams have not died. Their descendants, our generation, both men and women and even our youth, still share the same dreams. It is just a matter of each of us taking and doing our part in making those dreams a reality.

As I get more involved with communities, as I read the newspapers and listen to the television about sad events and stories, it is equally heart-warming and inspiring to hear individual efforts, different organizations' community programs, team-efforts, etc. *People are reaching out to others.* We all hope that the government can help, but people are not just sitting around and waiting anymore. We know that our government does not have all the answers to everything, and it needs our help too. So, people are now beginning to ask, *"What can I do?"* Or saying, *"I want to help, just let me know how."*

Each person has an important role or purpose in this life. Each special ability, gift or talent, is our contribution to compliment with the others, like the puzzle. Such contribution to society is *unique* to each individual. Meaning, whatever it is YOU suppose to do, you need to do or share, as *nobody else* can do it like you do.

Personally, I have said to myself several times, "If I can only finish this book, I will die fulfilled." Now that it is finished and I am still alive, it only means that my purpose is not done yet, that there are still more things to be done. It has been the purpose of this book to reach others and to help them gain awareness, gain hope and courage to go on, to move on with a better perspective or outlook in life. I believe that *each person*, even those who seem hopeless, has *something good inside* them. There are still talents, potentials and valuable resources that remain untapped. It is my sincere desire that even just one or two people may be touched or helped by this book, it will be all worth it.

Going around in the community, I see or meet people with young children lining up on a homeless shelter or food pantry, veterans on the streets begging for help or work, and looks of distress, confusion or expression of desperation on more and more people. I feel the urgency of need for us to take action, to find immediate solutions to meet the people's need in every areas of their lives.

Each day as I read the news or heard on television about someone committing suicide or killing somebody (for practically minor or no reason at all), it really bothers me. And worse now with numerous massacre-type killing of innocent lives in our schools and other public places (not isolated in America but also happening in other parts of the world). The *abounding depression and hopelessness* haunted me. More and more broken relationships, domestic violence, abortions, horrific crimes, conflicts and wars are happening that could have been prevented. The continuous growth of crime involving very young children (even sometimes being committed by someone close to them), all these things compelled me to go on. God's unchanging grace, bountiful mercy, and unfailing love continue to inspire me.

Yes, we may not be able to solve all our problems. I will be lying to you if I will not admit that if things don't change (if we do not do our part to make the change), the possibility of our society totally deteriorating, and our world headed for the worse, is great. This is a "WAKE UP" call. Do not confine your vision to yourself alone. Look around you. Remove those blindfolds, see and know what are truly going on. We are the true 'reality show.' Be assured that as people gain knowledge on how to live and survive, and learn to CARE again, whatever comes can be tackled. Those adversities should not rob us of the HOPE and the JOY that we deserve and can truly have.

There is **HOPE**... **H**ealth and
                       Opportunity for
                       People
                       Everywhere

I believe that someday, more and more people will find true happiness, better health and peace of mind. There will be opportunities for them to express their talents and be their best, more dreams realized, and finally, experience more VICTORIES in their lives.

"Somewhere out there is a unique place for you to help others – a unique role for you to fill that only you can fill."

– Thomas Kinkade, American artist

Together Making A Difference

"In helping others, we shall help ourselves, for whatever good we give out completes the circle and comes back to us."

— Flora Edwards, author, writer

The situation we now face as a society can be summarized into four thoughts, and what we can do about it:

1. We have lost track of the real VALUES in life, including moral and family values. We need to go back to our basic character molding for wellness.

2. We focus more on the 'cure' (of health problems, what to do with the sick, the criminals, the homeless, etc.) instead of putting more attention on PREVENTION.

3. We have become total strangers, not trusting or even knowing our own neighbors. We need to GET BACK TO EACH OTHER, get to know one another, share our concerns and ideas.

4. We are so disintegrated, everyone is 'doing their own thing'. To find effective solutions, we need to learn to WORK TOGETHER, cooperate, collaborate, supportive of each other for healthier community. We do not need disasters or calamities to find ourselves needing each other, helping one another. This can be our WAY of LIFE.

WE CAN RECOVER! WE CAN REBOUND! WE CAN REBUILD! My vision shows people realizing that going back to basics is the only way to build a solid foundation for ourselves and for our society. To build a solid, strong, steady and stable foundation applies to an individual, a marriage, a family, a team, a community and a society. Just like building a house, it does not matter how big or fancy the house is, even with all the riches and latest technology on it, if it has a poor foundation it could crumble when a calamity (earthquake, hurricane, etc., natural or man-made) strikes. In the same way, that is how vulnerable an individual, a marriage, a family, a team, a community and even a society can be without a solid foundation. That is why there are people who appear to be all right, who have everything, even highly educated, and then in an instant, for various reasons, can become involved with drugs, divorce, suicide and violent crimes. Building a solid foundation starts from the base (back to basics). For an individual, this means 'meeting his basic needs first' in all six areas. For if there are six foundations and one or two are neglected, the house will still crumble.

A COMMUNITY or a SOCIETY cannot be expected to be well if the INDIVIDUALS are not well. Building a solid foundation does not work backward, like building from the roof down. If we wish to have a healthy and solid community and society, then we need to make the effort to care and provide for each individual's needs first. Once that is taken cared of, then the following can be expected:

more stable SOCIETY

⇧

more stable COMMUNITY

⇧

stronger TEAMS/GROUPS

⇧

stronger, stable FAMILIES

⇧

more stable, lasting MARRIAGE

⇧

a secure, stable INDIVIDUAL

In the process of our self-discovery as individuals and as a society, we are to remember OUR CHILDREN. Our beloved children are everywhere – at home, school, church, movie theaters, game stores, internet, etc. Our children learn from their parents, the teachers, church leaders, government and community leaders, the business owners, the movie industry leaders, the sports players, the movie and TV stars, and all the other adults who are their supposedly *role models*. Our children offer no excuses for our pure irresponsibility and misdoing (that is why rebellion of all forms comes). They are though very smart and forgiving to understand and accept that we adults are not perfect, provided they can see that we are sincerely doing our best. Instead of the home and school, even church and government, keep going back and forth on who has more responsibility in TEACHING our children, do remember that it takes a village, an entire community, to raise these children. If we don't get our acts together, if we do not learn that we need 'teamwork', working together to achieve better results, then we soon to be seniors will just have to watch and feel the consequences.

As we continue to share our dreams and visions, let us find a way to come back to each other, to build those strong foundations together. Be a brother, a sister, a neighbor, a friend. Let us also be A PARTNER to each other. Let us be actively involved with our schools, churches and communities, even on governing bodies related discussion. WE can learn to be 'team players' again – the team of people who care, the real WINNING TEAM!!!

> *"There is enough in the world for everyone to have plenty to live on happily and to be at peace with his neighbors."*
>
> – Harry S. Truman

> *"Until he extends the circle of his compassion to all living things, man will not himself find peace."*
>
> – Albert Schweitzer, Alsatian theologian, philosopher, physician, and musician

Let us bring HOPE to our community...

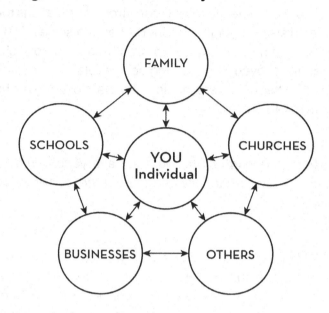

Be a PARTNER!

If we can only bring individuals, families, schools, churches, businesses and other segments of our community to work-together, it will make a world of difference for all of us.

What Can be Done?

Individually and collectively, it is time to realize that our planet Earth and everything with it is in a critical point. The world is changing, deteriorating rapidly before our eyes. We can no longer put on a blindfold, or be in denial about what's happening around us. We need to be proactive to face what's ahead of us. In real life, YOU and I are WE. Like it or not, ALL of US who inhabit our Earth are interconnected or interrelated. What can YOU and I, or WE, do?

1. More PUBLIC AWARENESS and open discussion of issues, problems, situations that affect us as individuals, families, society and as a nation.

2. Provide more HEALTH and TOTAL WELLNESS EDUCATION and FINANCIAL LITERACY for all age group.

3. Create more *comprehensive and integrated* COMMUNITY WELLNESS RESOURCE HUBS that people can call or go to in their community for information, education and training, for resources of various needs and support system addressing, not just one problem but, total wellness and financial security.

4. *Encourage more* EXPRESSIONS of DREAMS, TALENTS, CREATIVITIES among our children at home, at school, everywhere. Establish more schools, centers allowing plenty of space or room for them to explore to develop their God-given talents, personal development and character building, develop social skills to get along well with others, business and leadership orientation – so we don't only prepare our children for future careers but for better life in the future.

5. More SENIOR INDEPENDENT RETIREMENT COMMUNITIES with plenty of space, activities, care and opportunities to volunteer and be involved or contribute to our youth and community wellness.

6. Establish TRANSITION HOMES for the veterans and homeless people who may have lost their jobs or other circumstances, especially families with children, who just need a break and can use temporary support and encouragement, job skill or small business trainings and counseling to be able to successfully get back on their feet again.

7. Build more REHABILITATION or RESTORATION COMMUNITIES, instead of more jails, for minor or first time offenders, especially for the youth, equipped with education,

training and counseling programs to help individuals be more prepared to go back to the society and their families.

Life calls us to TAKE ACTION, positive, meaningful and productive action. Meaningful life comes from knowing that we are giving our best to live harmoniously with our Creator, with the others and with ourselves. '**Love God** *with all our being,' and* '**love others** *as we* **love ourselves'** are the only two things we need to remember and the rest of good things for each of us, for all of us will follow.

It is time for each of us, for our land, for our county to heal and be well again. When we align with God and His principles, work harmoniously with His plan for each of us and the environment we are in, we cannot go wrong. The energy forces within us and around us will bring that desire into reality. *"Come what may, the best of life is still to come!"*

> *"I expect to pass through life but once. If, therefore, there be any kindness I can show, or any good thing I can do to any fellow being, let me do it now, for I shall not pass this way again."*
> — William Penn, Founder of Pennsylvania, USA

The Final Call

Here is a very interesting story, true or not...

The Last Wishes of Alexander the Great - by an Unknown Author or Storyteller

This is a story of Alexander, the great Macedonian king. As everyone knows Alexander the Great had conquered almost the whole world by the time he was 32. He was unconquered and undefeated, making him one of the greatest kings in world history. Unfortunately on his way back home he developed an illness, which his physicians could not cure. With death staring him in his face, Alexander realized how his conquests, his great army, his sharp sword and all his wealth were of no consequence.

He was not afraid of death, but he wanted to see his mother before he died. The doctors were helpless. Alexander was ready to trade all the kingdoms, wealth and glory that he had amassed during his lifetime to see his home land and mother again. Unfortunately, they were in vain.

Alexander realized that all his conquests, wealth and glory wouldn't be of any help when he was to face death. They had no meaning to him anymore. They were useless. He realized that death will soon arrive and it was impossible to go back home. So, the mighty conqueror lay prostrate and pale, helplessly waiting to breathe his last.

He called his Commander and said, "I will depart from this world soon. I have three wishes. Please carry them out without fail." With tears rolling down his cheeks, the Commander agreed to abide by the king's last wishes.

Alexander said, "My first desire is that my physicians alone carry my coffin."

"Secondly, I desire that when my coffin is carried to the grave, the path leading to the graveyard be strewn with gold, silver and precious stones which I amassed during my conquests.

"My third and last wish is that both my hands be kept dangling out of my coffin."

The people wondered at the king's strange wishes. But no one dared to ask him. Alexander's favorite Commander kissed his hand and pressed them to his heart. "O king, we assure you that your wishes will all be fulfilled. But tell us why do you make such strange wishes?"

Alexander took a deep breath, smiled and said: "I would like the world to know of three lessons I have learned.

First, I wanted my physicians to carry my coffin because people should realize that no doctor on earth can really cure anyone. They are powerless and cannot save a person from the clutches of death. So let not people take life for granted. People should learn to treasure their lives.

The second wish of strewing riches on the way to the graveyard is, I want to tell people that not even a fraction of the gold that I had collected is going to come with me. I spent all my life earning riches but cannot take it with me. Let people realize that it is a sheer waste of time to chase wealth. I want people to learn from my mistakes.

My third wish to have my hands dangling out of the coffin is to let them know that I came empty handed into this world, and empty handed I will go out of this world." I can't even take my body along with me on this journey of death.

Alexander's last words: "*Bury my body, do not build any monuments, keep my hands outside so that the world would know that the person who won the world, had nothing in his hands when he died*".

With these words, the king closed his eyes. Soon he let death conquer him and breathed his last.

160

Another popular story you may already be familiar with...

A Story of Faith

A few days prior to the touch down of a heavy typhoon, residents were warned to prepare to evacuate to prevent disastrous consequences. A certain man claimed to have full faith (we will call him Joe) adamantly refused to heed the warning. First, a bus was sent to those who were still left behind in their houses. Joe still sat by the doorstep. He refused saying, "God is with me and will take care of me." As the water rose, he started going to the second floor and slept. When he awoke, he watched things going on outside. No one else was around. Then a rescue boat came by pleading with him to leave because the water was still expected to rise. Once again, he refused saying, "I'm not worried. God will take care of me." The boat left. The water started rising very fast that Joe was forced to hurry up to the rooftop. A helicopter shortly came by and yelled, "Joe, this is your last chance. Hurry, come now!" In spite of being cold in the pouring rain, he still refused and once again said, "I know God will take care of me." Needless to say, he drowned.

In Heaven, Joe confronted God, saying, "What happened? How could you abandon me and let me die when I had full faith in you?" God replied, "Joe, I didn't forget or abandon you. I sent you help many times. Remember the bus, the boat and the helicopter? You refused them all. What else could I have done?"

Moral of the story: Be sensitive to what God is really telling or giving you, not just what you think. A lot of times help or opportunity is already in front of us, but we refuse to see or realize its presence and value.

As we close, may you allow me to share what I now know, believe, and conclude…

TIME is gold. HEALTH is wealth. KNOWLEDGE is treasure. This truly is an old time wisdom which remains applicable as ever.

There is One true God who is made known through His magnificent creations, nature and including us. We are to worship Him in Spirit and in Truth. We are in this world, but not of this world. That's how I learned to live *outside the box*. God did not intend for us to be just confined in the box.

We do not have to conform with the limitations imposed to us by this world or society, such as pressure to be politically correct, to oblige, to compromise. But we are to be transformed by the renewing of our mind to what is just and right in the eyes of both God and humankind. To live with true freedom is to be able to take the responsibility to stand on something we can believe in.

It is TIME… It is time to WAKE UP! It is time to face the truth, make your wise decision as this may be your last chance. It is time to face realities and make a stand.

Something BIG is Happening… When I wrote the original *Today's S.O.S.* about twenty years ago, for some reason I couldn't come up with a closing title or ending statement. So, I just titled it ***"Now, What's Next"*** – This is not the end, but just the beginning. Same thing happened for the next books that followed. That must be for the long rugged road journey I've been through… to witness, and be able to testify of, life here on Earth.

This one is different. As I think of possible ending or conclusion, this came to me: ***"The Last Chapter."*** It surprised me for a while. Then, I opened myself to the possibilities and started writing as thoughts flow in me.

At one point I stopped and remembered daring to ask, "God, are you sure you want this for my ending?" Yes, is the definite answer.

I wouldn't object. My job is to trust and obey. I also thought that the chapter might be pertaining to the coming ending of my life or my life's story on Earth. It gave me so much peace and comfort that "Yes! I'm so ready to welcome that moment." Yes, I am certainly ready to receive that wonderful occasion… as nothing else on Earth could be better than "What's Next?" with my Creator.

As for Everyone, may He find you READY to receive Him who loves you, and prepared to spend the rest of everlasting time with Him, our Maker, our Abba Father, the true One Living God, the Lord of lords and the King of kings. All I know now is…

Something BIG is coming… happening…
Are you READY?

Now here's the *ultimate test*, which determines the health state of your spirit and mind:

Are you at peace and see this as something healthy
and positive – that something good or wonderful
is about to happen, and you can rejoice!

OR

You have an uncomfortable feeling of uncertainties and anxieties?

Then, it is TIME to make up your mind, remembering that the CHOICE and DECISION you make from here on will greatly affect the rest of your LIFE, on Earth and beyond.

(Continue reading… don't miss Mother Teresa's poem *"Do It Anyway"* and the *"Declaration"*)

Are you ready? The answer must be **"Yes!"** As we can make this popular phrase a true reality, ***"And we together lived happily ever after."*** Survive and thrive in our time because you can, now you know it is possible. And once you prepared yourself for whatever comes, with peace that passes all understanding, look forward for the best that yet to come.

God bless you and us all!

*And in the end it's not the years in your life that count.
It's the life in your years.*

– Abraham Lincoln

Life is a promise; fulfill it.

– Mother Teresa

Someone gave this copy to me a long time ago and I still read it often as a source of guidance and inspiration. Let me share it with you...

Do It Anyway!

People are often unreasonable, illogical, and self-centered;
Forgive them anyway.
If you are kind, people may accuse you of ulterior motives;
Be kind anyway.
If you are successful, you will win some false
friends and some true enemies;
Be successful anyway.

– Mother Teresa

The BOOK of LIFE contains living words that can set you **FREE,** and help you live an **abundant** and **victorious life:**

"And you shall know the truth, and the truth shall make you free."

John 8:32

"The thief (enemy) *does not come except to steal, and to kill, and to destroy. I have come that they may have life, and that they may have it more abundantly."*

John 10:10

"For God so loved the world that He gave His only begotten Son, that whoever believes in Him should not perish but have everlasting life."

John 3:16

"Jesus said to him, *'I am the way, the truth, and the life. No one comes to the Father except through Me'."*

John 14:6

"For you did not receive the spirit of bondage again to fear, but you received the Spirit of adoption by whom we cry out, "Abba, Father." The Spirit Himself bears witness with our spirit that we are children of God"

Romans 8:16

"Jesus said to him, *'You shall love the Lord your God with all your heart, with all your soul, and with all your mind.' This is the first and great commandment. And the second is like it: 'You shall love your neighbor as yourself."*

Matthew 22:37

"And we know that all things work together for good to those who love God, to those who are the called according to His purpose."

Romans 8:28

"For we do not wrestle against flesh and blood, but against principalities, against powers, against the rulers of the darkness…."

Ephesians 6:12

"Yet in all these things we are more than conquerors through Him who loved us"

Romans 8:37

"Fear not, for I am with you; do not be dismayed, for I am your God. I will strengthen you, Yes, I will help you, I will uphold you with My righteous right hand."

Isaiah 41:10

"…if you have faith as a mustard seed, you will say to this mountain, 'Move from here to there,' and it will move; and nothing will be impossible for you."

Matthew 17:20

"But seek first the kingdom of God and His righteousness, and all these things shall be added to you."

Matthew 6:33

Believe! Be a mountain mover!

Declaration

This could be one of the most important steps that you will take in your life. If the *words* you say, and *believe with all your heart and mind*, determine the results that can affect your life, then *so be it*. Today, you can make *a personal declaration*.

A *declaration* is a formal statement or proclamation just like what the government, judicial or church officials do, like the *Declaration of Independence*. Today, you can reclaim your best life intended for you by making a declaration to yourself and to the world. Below is a sample.

You can do this best by going back to your mirror. It may be uncomfortable or seems silly at first, but as you take your life more seriously and have a great anticipation of what is about to come to you, you will find this declaration a very meaningful event in your life. Read first, repeat the process until you internalize the words, and eventually the words will come out naturally with your full belief and passion. That is when you are ready. ARE YOU READY???

I declare that...

I have the truth, and therefore, I am now FREE!

I am more than special, marvelously created and unique.

I am no longer allowing this world's thief to steal my joy and peace, nor to destroy my relationships and good future. I declare to receive the abundant life that is intended for me.

I accept that God loves me, believe and accept His Son as my Lord and Savior and the everlasting life He promised.

I am no longer in bondage of fear. Instead, I will live in the bond of God's love, my Abba, Father, for me. I know that all things will work together for good for me. I will live with purpose and my life will be lived to the fullest.

I am more than conqueror through Him who loves me!

I am victorious and I am ready to move mountains!

Signed: _____ Date: _____

Acknowledgement

Thank you to my Publishing Consultant, Erin Cohen, my Maketing Consultant, Will Roberts, my Check-in Coordinator, Rowella Alvaro, my Publishing Service Associate, Allen Endrina and my Designer Lloyd Micaros for helping me.

About the Author

Meet Anolia...

Anolia Orfrecio Facun, Community Wellness Advocate, Author, Speaker, Social Entrepreneur, Total Wellness Coach

Anolia is an active community health and wellness advocate. She is a former public health nurse (R.N., B.S.N.) turned successful entrepreneur in three separate industries (Health, Finance, Real Estate), to a passionate author and inspiring speaker with a story and a mission to share, ...the message of HOPE, LOVE and VICTORY in today's ailing world.

Anolia is the author of Amazon bestseller book, **Yes! The Secrets Work** – *Discover Your Unlimited Potential and Purpose in Life;* **Aloha The Message of Hawaii;** **The Spirit of Silicon Valley**, *Journeys and Transformations Beyond Technology; and the latest,* **Today's S.O.S**. *-Secrets of Survival and Ultimate Victory in Life; and more...*

Contact direct at: (808)282-7358
anolia@lcLIFEwell.com
www.yesthesecretswork.com

Emergency contact numbers and other resources:

9-1-1 - Fire, Police and Paramedics (life threatening situations)

2-1-1 - Any other non-emergency resources & support line, by **United Way**. When you do not know who to call, this connects you with hundreds of community services, 24 hrs. a day, including info and referrals for basic needs, child & elder care, counseling, employment, health, immigration assistance, volunteering, etc.

www.ready.gov – for more earthquake, emergency and disaster preparedness information

1-888-995-HOPE(4673) – **Homeownership Preservation Foundation** can help when facing **Foreclosure**, HUD certified. Or visit **www.995hope.org**.

1-866-557-2227 – **NFCC/Homeowner Crisis Resource Center** available in your area. Or visit **www.housinghelpnow.org**

1-800-388-2227 – **National Foundation for Credit Counseling.** Or visit **www.debtadvice.org**. Providing Debt Management Plan

1-800-222-1222 – **Poison Control** Center (24 hours; call 911 for emergencies)

1-800-342-2437 – **Communicable Disease Control & Prevention**

1-800-222-3463 – **Missing Children** Hotline

1-800-344-6000 – **Child Abuse** Hotline (Children Services Bureau)

1-800-799-7233 – National **Domestic Violence** Hotline

1-800-479-3339 – **Suicide and Crisis Intervention** (24 hrs.)

1-800-772-1213 – **Social Security** Office

1-800-500-6411 – **Women, Infants and Children** (WIC Program)

1-800-638-2772 – US **Consumer Product Safety** Commission Hotline

1-800-669-4000 – US **Equal Employment Opportunity** Commission

1-800-448-3543 – **American Red Cross** Blood Services

When you or someone you know need help, do not wait nor hesitate. There are help available. Avoid scams. Contact the mentioned resources first. Ask for referrals when necessary. Also check your local phone book for **Salvation Army, Local Food Pantries/Second Harvest** for immediate temporary help. It also contains **First Aid & Survival Guide** and many other emergency and helpful service numbers that you can call. Please advise us of other resources and groups or services that you find recommendable so we may add on our list.

Thank you!

Printed in the United States
By Bookmasters